Around the World in 100 Miles

World Cuisine Recipes with Local New England
Ingredients, Plus Poetry, Folklore, and Facts on Four Harvests

Created by Melissa Guillet

Sacred Fools

AROUND THE WORLD IN 100 MILES

Grateful Acknowledgment is given to the authors
whose work first appeared in the following forms:

Winter Baldwins by Joyce Heon, from her chapbook
<u>Winter Keeping Apples</u>.
How to Make Bread in 12 Steps by Ryk McIntyre.

Layout, Design, and Photography by Melissa Guillet
Text Set in BlairMdITC TT, Minion Pro, Optima and Times New Roman

ISBN 978-0-9845072-1-4 pbk.

Published by Sacred Fools Press
100milecookbook.blogspot.com
aroundtheworldin100miles.blogspot.com

Dedication

Special thanks to my brother-in-law, whose dietary restrictions got me thinking. Warm gratitude to my family for joining me in creating this book and for being guinea pigs trying all the recipes. Thanks to the actual guinea pigs and the chickens, for providing fertilizer for the garden. And thank you, readers, for seeking to cook with local ingredients.

CONTENTS:

Foreword

This collection features seasonal recipes for a truly fickle growing locale: New England. Whether your aim is to eat locally, eat healthier, become closer to nature, or have gluten-free options, this book has it. Eating seasonally also reduces your carbon footprint by minimizing shipping, packaging, and travel costs. Atop each recipe is a quick alert for gluten free, sulfite-free, vegetarian, vegan, and/or foraged or wild options.

But why eat only for sustenance? Embedded in this collection are facts about where food comes from – whether you are growing it yourself or purchasing it at a farmers' market – its folklore and history, and poetic interpretation of the rituals of preparing and enjoying food. Many ingredients are used in their unpackaged, unprepared form to reduce landfill waste and produce a fresher, healthier meal. Suggestions are also given on uses of certain recipes for seasonal occasions, such as "money bags" for Chinese New year, cranberry chutney in a baked brie for winter solstice or apple pie for the autumnal equinox. So enjoy, eat well, share a poem at the table, and dig in to what the earth has to offer.

~ Melissa Guillet

These Are a Few of My Favorite Things

We all have our favorite tools when we cook. Although it's not necessary to own or go and purchase these items to use this cookbook, they have come in handy and saved me time. Most cost less than $10 apiece if you shop around. So here is the list:

Box Grater. It has four different grating sides and saves on cooking time. Wash immediately after use to avoid cleaning stuck-on food on sharp edges.

Japanese chef knife. It's comfortable, rocks well, and stays sharp!

Kitchen shears. Finely-cutting fresh herbs without tearing the leaves or having cilantro this way and that is much easier simply snipping what you need into a measuring cup or spoon.

Micrograter. Great for mincing ginger and garlic, and zesting citrus fruits. Clean immediately after use.

Pastry cutter. Mine is flat with a rolled side, the cutting side marked with inches. This is helpful for measuring dough, but can also chop food and scoop it up to add to a pan. I use it most frequently for transporting diced onions.

Stainless-steel pans, including Dutch oven/sauté pan with lid. Stainless steel heats evenly, cleans easily, and unlike non-stick pans, will not potentially poison you. A lid lets you steam and cook as well as sauté.

The Basics

Basic Buttermilk Pancakes
Taste of Scotland

Prep: 5 minutes Cook: 10-15 minutes Makes ten 4" pancakes

1 egg
3/4 cup buttermilk
2 tbs. vegetable oil
1 cup unbleached flour
2 tsp. sugar
2 tsp. baking powder
1/2 tsp. salt

Beat egg in medium-sized bowl. Whisk in buttermilk and oil. Add remaining ingredients and beat until smooth. Let batter sit 10 minutes to activate baking soda. Preheat cast iron or stainless steel pan on medium, until water droplets sizzle. Pour about 1/8 cup of batter onto buttered pan, working in a circle and adding a center pancake if room allows. Cook about 5 minutes per side, turning once.

Variations:
Winter: Add 1 tsp. cinnamon or vanilla, 1/2 cup frozen berries or canned apples, pears, or peaches.
Spring: Add 1/2 cup thinly sliced rhubarb and strawberries.
Summer: Add 1/2 cup blueberries or skinless peach diced 1/2" with a dash of ground ginger.
Fall: Add 1/2 cup cooked or canned pumpkin or buttercup squash and 1/4 tsp. cinnamon or fresh ground nutmeg, or 1/2 cup processed, ground acorns (See page 134.)

Sweet or Savory Crêpes
Taste of France

Prep: 5 minutes Cook: 10-15 minutes Makes about six crêpes

1 egg
3/4 cup unbleached flour
1/4 cup wheat flour
1 3/4 cups milk
1 tbs. oil
1 tsp. sugar
Dash of salt
1 tsp. cinnamon (optional)

In a nonstick or cast iron pan, heat a small amount of oil over medium-low. Whisk egg, then beat in remaining ingredients until smooth. Pour batter half a cup at a time into pan and turn pan to form a thin circle. Cook for 3-5 minutes (less for each subsequent crêpe), then flip and cook other side for about 3 minutes. Serve with pure maple syrup or brown sugar, tucking in sides, then rolling crêpe.

Variations:
Late Spring/Summer: Stuff with strawberries and farmer's cheese, or omit sugar and stuff with sautéed vegetables, especially asparagus.
Late Summer/Fall: Stuff with blueberries and sour cream.
Fall/Winter: Stuff with cooked apple slices or apple sauce.

Gluten-Free Granola Bars
Taste of Earth

Prep: 15 minutes Cook: 30 minutes Makes 24 bars

1 cup All-Purpose Gluten-Free Flour*
1 1/2 cups oatmeal
1 cup cornmeal
1 cup berries (dried, frozen, or fresh – wild option:
    autumn olives or wild blueberries)
1/2 cup add-ins (i.e. shaved coconut, nuts, flax seed,
    mini chocolate chips, sunflower seed)
1/4 cup oil
1/2 cup brown sugar
1/2 cup molasses
local honey (optional)

Mix dry ingredients and berries in a large bowl. Stir in oil, sugars, and add-ins. Spread batter on greased 10"X14" baking dish and bake at 350°F for 30 minutes. Optional: Drizzle honey over batter during last five minutes of cooking. Cut bars while still warm. Remove when cool. Refrigerate.

* such as Bob's Red Mill or King Arthur brands.

Basic Pie Dough
Taste of Europe

Prep/Chill: 30 minutes Makes two 9" double-crust pies

2 cups unbleached flour
2 cups whole wheat flour
2 tsp. sugar
1 tsp. salt
1 tsp. coriander (optional)
1 3/4 cups vegetable shortening or lard
1 teaspoon cider vinegar
1 egg (or 1/4 cup oil for vegan recipe)
1/2 cup water

Sift together flours, sugar, salt, and coriander, if using. With fork, cut shortening into dry mixture. In a separate bowl, whisk together vinegar, egg or oil, and water. Combine the two mixtures, stirring with a fork until all ingredients are moistened. With floured hands, mold dough into four balls. Chill at least fifteen minutes before rolling. Dough can be kept wrapped in plastic in refrigerator for three days or frozen six months.

Basic Pizza Dough
Taste of Italy

Prep: 15 minutes Rise: 40 minutes Cook: 20 minutes
Makes 1 large pizza or two small.

2 tsp. yeast
2 tbs. olive oil
1 cup warm water or whey
1 cup whole wheat flour
1 1/2 cups unbleached flour
1 tsp. salt

This makes a stiffer dough than most, but holds up well to numerous toppings. Dissolve yeast in warm liquid. Add olive oil. Sift flours and salt into a medium bowl. Make a well in flour mixture and add liquid. Mix well with spoon, then knead on floured surface 3 minutes. Return to bowl and cover with hot damp towel. Let rise 40 minutes. Preheat oven (and pizza stone, if using) to 425°F. Roll dough out on floured surface. (Divide dough first if making two pizzas.) Transfer dough with two thin cutting boards or spatulas to pizza stone sprinkled with corn meal or to baking sheet. Add toppings and bake 15-20 minutes, until edges start to brown.

Variations:

Winter Pizza: Canned or frozen sauce or bruschetta, Swiss chard, mozzarella

Spring Pizza: Asparagus and mushrooms, queso blanco

Summer Pizza: Slice large tomato as thin as possible. Arrange slices on dough already on baking surface. (Juice from fresh tomatoes can make dough soggy until cooked.) Drizzle with olive oil. Top with crumbled feta cheese, such as Narragansett Creamery Salty Feta. Sprinkle with pepper. Top with fresh basil leaves. Bake 15-20 minutes at 425°F.

Fall Pizza: Spinach and goat feta

Calzone: Roll out a 6" round. Spread one side with sautéed vegetables, sauce, and/or cooked meat. Fold other side over. Brush with egg whites for shine. Bake as above.

How to Bake Bread in 12 Steps

by Ryk McIntyre

1. Don't even try this for decades. Fear the process.

2. Don't listen to Step 1. It had to go first. It has issues.

3. Start mixing the ingredients. Realize you don't have everything you need. Rush to the store in a panic. You're driving all over town on your birthday just so you can have cake. Stop. Breathe.

4. Just to be daring, just to be totally crazy, this one time in your life, try following the directions.

5. Suspect the recipe is lying to you. It wants you to fail. There is no way that much water is enough for all that flour. You should have listened to your parents when they told you to go into computers. How will you tell them you were wrong now?

6. Discover your sweet tears are just what the yeast needed to feed on. Add enough damn water until dough forms into a ball. Roll yourself into a ball. Rock gently.

7. Next, spread some flour on a cold, dry surface. This is so you don't leave fingerprints...

8. Fashion the dough into a form that approximates whoever it was that hurt you this bad. Add two fists. Add two, angry fists as much as you need. Your feelings are valid, damn it!

9. Let it go. Let it rest. Let the dough rest, too. For at least a half-hour. By then it will drop its guard... there's no way you're done venting.

11

10. You know why resentment is like fine wine?
They both age well, but with resentment you can get drunk on the same bottle, over and over. Now show the dough that Step 8 was just a stroll through Sunny Lollipop Land, compared to what's next. Regress 800 years; get Medieval on it.

11. Weep for all your sins and past disappointments. Stop blaming everything else for your failures. Remember to stop blaming yourself. Remember also that you should have already pre-heated the oven to 425 degrees, but it's Ok, it's no big deal, it'll just take a few minutes more. Take your therapist off speed-dial.

12. Divide the dough into two equal parts. Call both of them "The Future" because that's the only thing we can work towards. Today is a gift, that's why it's called the Present. Feel free to smack the crap out of anyone who says something that stupid to you while you're in pain. Place the loaves in the oven for 35 minutes. Use that time to transform some of the hurt you were sure you could never change. Make it into something that can feed not just you, but even people you don't know, body and soul. Then give yourself some credit... you did it. You survived. You made bread. This will be easier next time.

Irish Soda Bread
Taste of Ireland

Prep: 15 minutes Cook and Cool: 2 hours Makes one loaf

1 1/2 cups whole wheat flour
2 cups unbleached flour
1/2 cup wheat germ
1 tsp. salt
1 tsp. baking soda
1/3 cup unsalted butter (3/4 stick) (or vegan alternative)
2 cups buttermilk (or soy milk plus 1 tsp. cider vinegar)
1 tbs. molasses
1/2 cup rolled oats

Preheat oven to 400°F. Whisk together flours, wheat germ, salt, and baking soda. Cut butter into 1/2" cubes, then work into flour with a fork into a coarse meal. Create a well in the center and stir in buttermilk, molasses, and rolled oats until a dough forms. Generously flour hands and counter, and knead dough about three minutes. Place dough on greased sheet. (Traditionally, an "X" is cut a 1/2" deep across surface of dough.) Bake until golden brown and bread sounds hollow when bottom is tapped, about 45 minutes. Cool on rack, right side up, at least an hour. Store at room temperature in bread bag or plastic wrap, up to four days.

Multigrain Bread
Taste of Earth

Prep: 25 minutes Rise: 3-5 hours Bake 40-45 minutes
Cool: 1 hour Makes one loaf

1 1/2 cups bread flour
1 cup whole wheat flour
4 tsp. vital wheat gluten
1/2 cup oatmeal
1/2 cup multigrain cereal (such as Bob's Red Mill)
1 tsp. salt
1 1/4 cup warm water (100°F-115°F), divided
3 tsp. active dry yeast
1/4 tsp. sugar
2 tbs. olive oil
1/4 cup local honey (or substitute brown sugar)

In a large bowl, whisk together first six ingredients. Dissolve yeast with sugar into 1/4 cup of warm water in a separate bowl. Let sit about ten minutes, until foamy. Incorporate remaining water, oil, and honey, then make a well in the flour mixture and stir wet into dry. Flour hands and counter and knead bread about 10 minutes, until elastic. Place rounded 6" X 4" dough back in bowl and cover with hot wet towel. (I use my turned-off oven as a proofer.) Let rise 2-6 hours, or until dough has doubled. Grease bread pan and punch dough down. Transfer dough to bread pan, reshaping if needed. Let rise 1-2 more hours. Preheat oven to 350°F. Bake bread 40-45 minutes, until golden brown and hollow-sounding when tapped. Cool one hour.

Seasonal Frittata
Taste of Italy

Prep: 10 minutes Total Cook Time: 50-80 minutes Serves six

1 cup of chopped leafy greens, sprouts, or vegetables
1 medium yellow onion, diced
6 large eggs
1 cup fresh grated cheese
1 tbs. dried basil, marjoram, oregano, or thyme
1/2 tsp. salt
1/2 tsp. cayenne
oil for cooking

This is a great way to use up leftovers or small amounts of vegetables. Heat one tbs. oil in oven-safe stainless steel pan or cast-iron skillet. Sauté onions until translucent. Add vegetables and cook until soft or wilted. Loosely beat eggs in large bowl and stir in cheese, dried herbs, salt, and cayenne. Pour into pan with onions. Cook over med-low heat until almost set, 10-15 minutes. Place pan in oven and broil 1-3 minutes to brown.

Winter: Swiss Chard and Parmesan
Spring: Beet Greens, Mushrooms, and Goat Cheese
Summer: Tomato, Fresh Oregano
Fall: see "Carnival Gold Frittata" (page 144)

First the crocus and snowdrops, then the forsythia, daffodils, and hyacinth. Soon, the tulips and cherry tree. Morning filled with bird song. Frosty mornings and warm afternoons. Tentative plantings of peas and kale. Sorting seeds for May. Cleaning out the winter clutter. Setting goals and planning projects for the warmer weather ahead. Waiting for opportunities to burst forth like tiny green buds and shoots.

What's in Season: Apples (stored) • Arugula • Asparagus • Bok Choy • Carrots • Celeriac • Collards • Cranberries • Dried Fruit • Fiddeheads • Frozen Fruit • Frozen Vegetables • Garlic • Garlic Chives • Granola • Honey • Kale • Lettuce • Maple Syrup • Microgreens • Mushrooms (fresh and dried): Crimini, Oyster, Portabella • Nettles • Nuts • Onions • Parsnips • Pea Greens • Potatoes • Potted Herbs • Ramps • Rhubarb • Salad Greens • Shallots • Sprouts • Strawberries • Turnips

S P R I N G

• Winter Squash • Dairy: Cheese (cow, goat) • Eggs (chicken, duck, goose) • Milk (cow, goat) • Yogurt (cow, goat) • Meat: Beef • Chicken • Duck • Fowl • Goat • Lamb • Pork • Turkey • Seafood: Bluefish • Butterfish • Cod • Crab • Flounder • John Dorian • Haddock • Littleneck Clams • Lobster • Mackerel • Monkfish • Mussels • Oysters • Pollock • Quahogs • Scallops • Sea Bass • Sea Robins • Seaweed • Shrimp • Skate Wings • Squid • Steamers • Striped Bass • Swordfish • Tuna

What to Do: Plant a Tree • Start a Compost Pile • Forage for Dandelion Greens, Fiddleheads, and Ramps • Make Dyes from Beets, Onion Skins, and Other Natural Materials (Boil Gently with Vinegar) for Eggs • Hang Blown-Out Eggs on Tree • Have a Camouflage Egg Hunt • Look for Spring Peepers and Salamanders • Give a Spring Bouquet • Plant an Extra Row for a Food Pantry • Clean Out Hair Brushes and Leave the "Nests" Out For the Birds

Salads, Sides, and Soups

Spring Salad
Spring Rolls
Radish: Five Fresh Fixes
Radish Raita
Radish Rhubarb Relish
Kebabs with Radish Paratha
Rhubarb Compote
Rhubarb Pickles
Red Red Roots
Creamed Spinach
Creamy Cold Rhubarb Soup
Strawberry Soup
Yum Yum Soup

Spring Salad
Taste of France

Serves 4

Mesclun greens
2 oz. goat cheese
1/4 cup chopped walnuts
8 asparagus stalks
8 strawberries, washed, stemmed, and sliced
Wild option: chickweed and young dandelion greens
1/3 cup balsamic vinegar
1/3 cup local honey

Combine vinegar and honey in a microwave-safe dish. Microwave one minute. Set aside. Wash and dry greens. Break off woody stems from asparagus and break or cut into bite-sized pieces. Saute in cast-iron skillet or broil in oven, 2-3 minutes, until tender-crisp and slightly browned. Set aside. Toast walnuts in cast iron skillet with some of the honey/vinegar mix 2-3 minutes. Divide greens on four plates. Top with walnuts, asparagus, and sliced strawberries. Using a fork, crumble goat cheese over top. Drizzle with dressing. Serve immediately.

Spring Rolls
Taste of Vietnam

Prep: 15 minutes   Makes 15 rolls

2 oz. rice vermicelli
16 chinese cabbage leaves or 1 cup mixed salad greens
8 mint leaves, plus garnish (lemon balm also works)
3 tbs. cilantro
3 (wild) chive stems
1 carrot, grated
2 radish, grated
1 stalk of rhubarb, sliced fine
2 tsp. white sugar
2 tbs. white vinegar
1 cup small local cooked shrimp, chopped (optional)
15 rice wrappers

Chop cabbage or greens, herbs, and scallions fine. Combine with other vegetables, sugar, and vinegar. Boil rice vermicelli until soft, drain, and cool with cold water. Drain again and cut into inch-length pieces using kitchen shears. Mix well with vegetables (and shrimp, if using). Soak rice wrappers in warm water in a pie dish, one at a time for about 30 seconds. Place about half a cup of mixture near top of the corner of the wrapper, fold over, and roll tightly. Tuck in sides half-way through rolling, and roll until end. Serve chilled, with mint leaves for garnish.

Radish

Five Fast Fresh Fixes

Grated Radish: Add to salads, soups, or pizzas.

White Radish Slaw: Grate one bunch of radishes (about 1/4 cup). Mix with 1/2 tsp. each of sugar and apple cider vinegar.

Radish Butter: Grate and mix with butter, heat gently, then chill in refrigerator. Spread on toasted bagels or rye bread.

Radish Hummus: Add to hummus. Use as veggie dip or spread.

Radish Cream Cheese: Mix grated radish with cream cheese. Serve on toasted bagel with local smoked blue fish.

Radish Raita
Taste of India Meets Greece

Prep: 15 minutes   Makes about one cup

1/2 cup firm, trimmed radishes, grated
1/4 cup feta goat cheese
3/4 cup Greek yogurt
1 tsp. fresh curry leaves, chopped
3 tsp. mint, chopped
1/8 tsp. black pepper

Combine all ingredients and run through food processor or blender. Spread on bagel with smoked salmon or local smoked blue fish, in a wrap with mixed greens or sprouts, or fill cucumber sandwiches. My daughter eats it by the spoonful.

Radish Rhubarb Relish
Taste of India

Prep: 10 minutes Cook: 20 minutes Chill: overnight

1/2 cup radish, grated
1/2 cup rhubarb, sliced 1/4" thick
1/4 cup carrot, peeled and grated
1/2 cup red onion, finely diced
3/4 cup cider vinegar
3/4 cup white sugar
1/2 tsp. salt

Mix all ingredients well. Bring mixture to boil in small sauce pan. Boil gently until liquid is reduced by half, about 20 minutes. Chill overnight to develop full flavors. Serve as a garnish, in a wrap with lettuce and grilled vegetables, or on grilled chicken, burgers, hot dogs, or vegan alternatives. This recipe has not been tested for canning. Keep refrigerated and use within two weeks.

Kebabs with Radish Paratha
Taste of India

Prep: 30 minutes Marinate: overnight Cook: 20 minutes Serves 4

Marinade:
2 tbs. olive oil
2 tbs. lemon juice
1 tsp. curry
1/2 tsp. garlic powder
1/2 tsp. cumin
salt and pepper to taste

Kebabs: 1 lb. lamb, chicken, squirrel, onion, potato, and/or cauliflower, cut into bite-size chunks

Soak bamboo skewers at least thirty minutes. Cut meat and/or vegetables into bite-sized pieces and marinate in refrigerator overnight. Pierce pieces with soaked bamboo skewers and place on broiling pan or cookie sheet. Broil about 4 minutes per side, checking that chicken is cooked through, if using. Potatoes will need about 8 minutes per side.

Parathas:
1 cup unbleached flour
1/2 cup whole wheat flour
1/8 tsp. salt
2 tbs. oil
1/3 cup warm water
1/2 cup grated radish

Whisk together dry ingredients. Make a well and mix in oil and water. Knead into a soft dough. Form four balls and roll dough into rounds. Sprinkle each round with radish. Fold rounds into quarters and roll 1/2 inch thin. Cut into smaller triangles, if desired. In large skillet or cast iron pan, heat 2 tbs. cooking oil, turning pan to coat. Cook parathas 4-5 minutes a side, until slightly browned. Serve warm with vegetable, chicken or lamb kebabs. Parathas can be kept warm in an oven wrapped in foil.

Rhubarb Compote
Taste of France

Prep: 5 minutes Cook: 20 minutes

2 1/2 cups rhubarb, sliced 1/2" thick (about 5 stalks)
1/4 cup plus 2 tbs. water
1/4 cup brown sugar
1 tbs. local honey (optional)
2 tsp. corn starch
1/4 cup finely chopped walnuts
1 tsp. lemon zest

Dissolve corn starch with 2 tbs. water. Mix with all ingredients except nuts. Heat in a heavy saucepan over medium-high heat, stirring constantly, about 2 minutes. Reduce heat and simmer 10 minutes. Stir in nuts and cook 5 more minutes. Serve at room temperature or slightly chilled.

Rhubarb Pickles
Taste of Earth

Prep: 5 minutes* Cook: 10-15 minutes Makes 2 pints

1 1/2 cups white vinegar
3/4 cups sugar
7 whole cloves
1/4 tsp. crushed red pepper
10 stalks of rhubarb, cut to 3" lengths
2 pint-size mason jars

In small sauce pan, dissolve sugar into vinegar and bring mixture to boil. Add cloves and red pepper and simmer 10 minutes. Keep two sanitized mason jars in a bowl of hot water in preparation. Fill each jar with half the rhubarb stalks. Pour vinegar mixture over stalks and secure lids. (Leave a half-inch of space if canning. Can in hot water bath ten minutes.) For immediate use, let cool on towel on counter, then refrigerate overnight.

* Time does not include sterilizing jars.

Red Red Roots
Taste of Morocco

Prep: 15 minutes Cook: 20 minutes Serves six

4 organic beets, peeled and sliced into 1/4" rounds
4 organic carrots, peeled and sliced into 1/4" rounds
1 organic turnip, peeled, sliced, and cut into like-size
   pieces
1 tbs. butter
1 cup chicken or vegetable broth
1/2 cup brown sugar
1/2-3/4 tsp. cayenne pepper
1/4 cup red wine

Melt butter in cast iron or sauce pan over med-high heat. Add vegetables, coating with melted butter and letting beets "bleed" over and turn the dish red. Add broth, sugar, and cayenne pepper. Simmer until vegetables start to soften, about 10 minutes, stirring occasionally to allow sugar to glaze. Continue cooking, adding more broth or water to prevent sticking. End result should be a thick syrup. Deglaze pan with wine and cook five more minutes. Serve immediately.

Creamed Spinach
Taste of Britain

Prep: 5 minutes Cook: 10 minutes Serves six

2 tbs. butter
4 cloves chopped garlic
6 cups chopped baby spinach
1/4 cup whipping cream
1/2 tsp. salt
1/4 tsp. pepper
pinch of cayenne

Melt butter in sauce pan over med-high heat. Add garlic, stirring, 2-3 minutes. Add spinach and cook, covered, 3-5 minutes, or until spinach wilts. Slowly pour in cream and stir in seasonings. Reduce heat and simmer 2-3 minutes. Serve immediately.

Creamy Cold Rhubarb Soup
Taste of Norway

Prep: 5 minutes Cook: 12-15 minutes Serves six

5 rhubarb stalks, peeled (reserving peel for stock) and sliced
   1/4" thick
3 small pieces of cinnamon bark (or substitute cassia)
3 cups water
1/2 cup white sugar
1 tsp. chopped lemon thyme leaves, reserving stems
1 tsp. chopped mint leaves, reserving stems
1 cup buttermilk

Combine rhubarb peelings, cinnamon, sugar, herb stems, and water in medium sauce pan. Bring to boil. Reduce heat and simmer 10 minutes. Strain liquid into bowl, compost remaining solids, then return liquid to pan. Add rhubarb pieces, bring to boil again, then remove from heat. Stir in buttermilk. Cool completely. Serve cold, garnished with chopped mint.

Strawberry Soup
Taste of Poland

Prep: 5 minutes Cook: 3-5 minutes Serves four

1 pound strawberries, washed, hulled and sliced
1 tbs. confectionary sugar
1 tbs. corn starch
1/2 cup Greek yogurt
1/4 cup light sour cream, plus more for garnish
1 tsp. almond extract

Mix strawberries and sugar. Stir corn starch into mix until dissolved. Heat in small sauce pan slightly to soften berries and release juices. Remove from heat and blend with rest of ingredients with an immersion or standard blender. Serve chilled. Garnish with a dollop of sour cream. Makes four servings.

Yum Yum Soup
Taste of Thai

Prep: 10 minutes Cook: 25 minutes Serves six

2 tbs. olive oil
1 onion, diced
1/2 lb. asparagus and/or fiddleheads, cut bite-sized
1 Yukon Gold potato, cut into 1/2" cubes
2 tbs. fresh lemon thyme
2 cups seafood stock
2 cups coconut milk
1-2 lbs. seafood: smoked bluefish, dabs, flounder, smoked
  shark, and/or monkfish
salt and pepper to taste
red pepper flakes (optional)

Loosely based on Tom Yum soup, it's hearty enough as a main course. Heat oil over medium heat in a large stock pot. Sauté onions until translucent. Add asparagus and/or fiddleheads, cooking gently until tender-crisp. Add potatoes, thyme, stock, and coconut milk. Bring to gentle boil and simmer until potatoes are soft. Add seafood and cook until opaque. Season with salt and pepper and red pepper, if using.

Main Dishes

Turkey Burgers
Baked Bunny Bao
Chicken Pot Pie
Chicken Madeira

Turkey Burgers
Taste of Earth

Prep: 10 minutes Cook: 30 minutes Makes about 12 burgers

1 lb. lean ground turkey
1/2 yellow onion, diced
1 tbs. brown mustard (1 tsp. mustard powder for sulfite-free)
1 tsp. organic curry
1 tsp. garlic powder
salt and pepper to taste
2 tbs. olive oil, divided

Sauté onions in 1 tbs. olive oil over medium heat until translucent. In a large bowl, mix well with ground turkey and spices. Form into patties 3" in diameter and 1" thick. Cook in 1 tbs. olive oil over medium/low heat 8 minutes one side, 5-8 minutes on the other. Serve on toasted whole wheat rolls or for gluten-free/low-carb option, in a wrap with lettuce, tomato, and diced red onion.

Baked Bunny Bao

Taste of China Meets France

Prep: 40 minutes Rise: 40 minutes Bake: 20 minutes Makes 25-30

Bun:
4 cups unbleached flour
1 tsp. sugar
1 tsp. salt
4 tbs. unsalted butter, cut into 1/2" cubes
1 packet active dry yeast
1 cup milk
zest of one lemon

Hollandaise Sauce:
3 egg yolks (reserve whites for filling)
juice of one lemon
1 stick of unsalted butter, melted
1/8 tsp. salt
1/8 tsp. white pepper

Filling:
1/4 pound Black Forest ham, cut into 1" squares
1 egg plus egg whites, poached or fried and chopped
wild garlic chives, or six asparagus, finely chopped

Traditionally steamed, these Chinese buns are baked until just golden, adding a buttery crunch to the lemony dough and savory filling. For buns, sift together dry ingredients except for yeast. Cut in butter. Warm milk to 130°F on stove and dissolve yeast. Stir in lemon zest and add milk mixture to dry mixture, mixing until all flour is incorporated. Knead on floured surface until elastic, about 15 minutes. Return to bowl and cover with hot wet towel, about 40 minutes to let dough rise.

Pound down dough and form into a 3" diameter log. Cut into 25-30 1/2" slices and roll each slice into a 4" round. Divide ham, egg, and chives or asparagus between rounds. Add one tsp. of Hollandaise sauce to each, reserving the rest for dipping. Pinch each round closed, using a drop or two of water if dough won't stick. Turn bun over and gently push outer edges down to mold into an "egg" shape. For "bunnies", use kitchen or herb sheers to pinch two ears from center of bun toward first third of bun, careful not to cut through dough into filling. Make eyes by piercing dough with end of chopstick. Brush bunnies and/or eggs with melted butter. Bake on parchment or greased cooking tray at 425°F for 20 minutes. Serve on an assortment of edible greens and flowers, such as pea greens, asparagus, mesclun and dandelion greens, dill, violets, and nasturtiums.

To make Hollandaise sauce, have all ingredients ready. In double boiler or small sauce pan placed inside larger sauce pan filled with about 2" of water, heat water until barely simmering. Whisk yolk and lemon together, then add to boiler, whisking constantly until the thickness of custard, about 2 minutes. (Overheated yolks will scramble.) Gradually add melted butter, whisking rapidly after each addition. Remove from heat. Stir in salt and pepper. Best served immediately. If made ahead and refrigerated, warm in microwave 10 seconds at a time at 50% power.

Chicken Pot Pie

Taste of Medieval France

Prep: 30 minutes Cook: 40 minutes Serves six to eight

Pie Crust (see page 8)

3 tbs. olive oil, divided
1/2 tsp. each salt and white pepper
1 pound chicken tenders, cut into bite-sized pieces
1 cup carrots, peeled and cut 1/4" thick
2 stalks sliced celery or 1/2 cup grated celeriac
1/2 diced red onion
2 cloves garlic, minced
2 medium potatoes cut into 1/2" pieces
1/4 cup flour
1 cup chicken broth
1 cup milk
2 tsp. dried lemon thyme
1/4 cup fresh chopped parsley

Preheat oven to 350°F. Heat large sauté pan with 1 1/2 tbs. oil over medium-high heat. Season chicken with salt and pepper. Cook chicken in batches, turning 3/4 through cooking time. Set meat aside. Add remaining olive oil and cook carrots, celery, and onions until onions become translucent, about 5 minutes. Add garlic, cooking one minute. Stir in flour until vegetables are coated. Slowly pour in broth and milk, alternating between both. Bring to a gentle boil, then add potatoes.

Reduce heat to medium-low, cover, and cook ten more minutes. Meanwhile, roll out one or two rounds of pie crust. Check that potatoes are soft, then add chicken, lemon thyme, and parsley. Stir well. For double-crust, fold round in half twice to transfer to pie pan. Unfold and drape over edges. Pour pie filling into crust. For single crust, use non-stick spray in pie pan before adding filling. For top crust, fold other round twice to transfer to top of pie. Unfold and cut excess from top and bottom crusts as needed. Tuck upper crust edges under, pressing into lower crust. Edges can be pleated by hand or with a fork for a decorative effect. Cut five slits in crust like the points of a star. Cook 40 minutes. Let cool 10 minutes before slicing.

Chicken Madeira
Taste of Portugal

Prep: 10 minutes Cook: 25 minutes Serves six

1 1/2 lbs. chicken breast or tenders, cut bite-sized
1 cup baby bella (crimini) mushrooms, sliced
10 leaves of fresh, organic sage, finely chopped
1 cup chicken broth
1/2 cup Madeira wine
2 tbs. unbleached flour
2 tbs. unsalted butter
1 tbs. brown sugar
1/2 red onion, diced
1 tbs. olive oil
1/8 tsp. salt
1/8 tsp. plus 1 tsp. pepper

Trim fat and tendons from chicken. Placing wax paper on top of meat, pound chicken with a mallet until flattened by half. Cut into bite-sized pieces and sprinkle with 1/8 tsp. of salt and pepper. Heat oil in large sauté pan to med-high. Cook chicken through, about 4 minutes per side. Set aside. In same pan, melt butter and brown sugar. Add onion and cook one minute, stirring frequently. Pour in broth and wine. Whisk in flour. Add mushrooms, sage, and rest of pepper. Stir well. Bring to boil, then reduce to simmer 10 minutes, stirring occasionally. Return chicken to pan and stir in to warm chicken. Serve immediately with baked potato or pasta, asparagus or peas.

Treats

Rhubarb Goldberg Machine
Lavender Shortbread

Rhubarb Goldberg Machine
Taste of Earth

Prep: 10 minutes Cook: 25 minutes Makes twelve muffins

1/4 cup butter, melted
2 eggs
1 cup strawberry yogurt*
1/4 cup buttermilk
1 1/2 cup unbleached flour
1/2 cup white sugar
2 tsp. baking powder
1/2 tsp. salt
1 cup rhubarb stalks, sliced 1/4" thick*
1 cup old-fashioned oats
1/4 cup sliced almonds (optional)

This muffin has it all, but bakes light and fluffy. Melt butter. In a small bowl, whisk in eggs, then yogurt and buttermilk. Sift dry ingredients in large bowl. Mix rhubarb, oatmeal, and nuts into dry mix. Stir wet ingredients into dry until just moistened. Fill 12 greased muffin tins. Bake at 400°F 20-25 minutes.

* Substitute plain or other yogurt flavors depending on fruit selected. Try adding a teaspoon of vanilla or orange extract with autumn olives, blackberries, blueberries, cranberries, or strawberries, peeled apple or pear with cinnamon or ground ginger, pumpkin or zucchini with nutmeg, or (sour) cherries with almond extract and chocolate chips.

Lavender Shortbread
Taste of England

Prep: 10 minutes Chill: 30 minutes Cook: 10 minutes Makes app. 80

2 tbs. plus 1 tsp. fresh organic lavender flowers
1 stick of unsalted butter, cut into 1/2" cubes
2 tbs. local honey
1/2 cup confectioner's sugar
1 1/2 cups unbleached flour
2 tbs. lavender tea

With electric beater, blend chilled butter with 2 tbs. of lavender flowers, honey, and sugar. Make a tea with remainder of flowers and stems, pouring 1/4 cup of hot water over both in a mug and letting seep covered five minutes. Add half the flour to butter mixture gradually, alternating with tea, until crumbly. Blend in remainder of flour with a spoon, working it into a smooth dough. Roll in a wax paper log 1" thick. Chill 30 minutes.

Preheat oven to 325°F. Cut log into 1/2" inch slices. Bake on ungreased cookie sheet or parchment paper until just golden on the bottom, 10 minutes. (Cook longer for larger cookies.) Cool before handling. Store in airtight container.

At last, some reliably warm weather! Tomatoes are ripening. Butterflies and bees visit the many flowers. Time to start canning and drying, because it all ends so soon! Invite some friends over. Show them how to can. Trade your jars in the fall. Take time to relax. Share some wine. Enjoy the fire with marshmallows and fireflies. Count the chirps of crickets.

What's in Season: Apples (stored) • Arugula • Beets • Bok Choy • Broccoli • Brussels Sprouts • Cabbage • Carrots • Cauliflower • Celeriac • Chard • Cider • Collards • Dried Fruit • Frozen Fruit • Frozen Vegetables • Garlic • Granola • Honey • Kale • Leeks • Maple Syrup • Microgreens • Mushrooms (fresh and dried): Crimini, Oyster, Portabella • Nuts • Onions • Parsnips • Potatoes • Potted Herbs • Salad Greens • Shallots • Sprouts • Sweet Potatoes • Turnips • Winter Squash • Dairy: Cheese (cow, goat) • Eggs (chicken, duck, goose) • Milk (cow, goat) • Yogurt (cow, goat) • Meat: Beef

SUMMER

• Chicken • Duck • Fowl • Goat • Lamb • Pork • Turkey • Seafood: Butterfish • Cod • Crab • Flounder • Haddock • Littleneck Clams • Lobster • Mackerel • Monkfish • Mussels • Oysters • Pollock • Quahogs • Scallops • Sea Bass • Sea Robins • Seaweed • Shrimp • Skate Wings • Squid • Steamers • Striped Bass • Swordfish • Tuna • Wild: Blueberries • Blackberries • Chickweed •Concord Grapes • Fox Grapes • Mustard Greens • Raspberries

What to Do: Pick Berries • Can Fruit • Take a Nature Walk or Hike • Attend a Summer Festival • Go Quahogging • Photograph Fairies (Pollinating Insects) • Build a Sandcastle or Beached Mermaid • Enjoy Summer Reading • Make Ice Cream By Rolling Cream, Sugar, and Natural Flavors in a Coffee Tin Packed in a Larger Tin Insulated with Ice and Salt. 20 Minutes Later, Ice Cream! • Share Your Harvest with Neighbors and the Needy. • Fill a Nature Box: Decorate a Shoe Box for Outside Treasures • Collect, Sketch, and Release Bugs • Look Under Logs for Detrivores

Salads, Sides, and Soups

Honey Summer Salad
Garden Dressing
Catalina Dressing
Garlic Scapes
Parsley Sauce
Tomato Sauce
Zippy Zucchini
Baba Ganoush
Mock-A-Mole
Fiesta Muffins
Summery Succotash
Turnip: Four Fresh Fixes
Cabbage Cole Slaw
Coconut Cauliflower
Clam Cakes (Gluten-Free)
Birth of Venus Soup
Kale Soup

Honey Summer Salad
Taste of Many Places

Dressing:
1 clove garlic, minced
2 tsp. brown mustard
2 tbs. cider vinegar
2 tbs. walnut oil
2 tbs. local honey

Salad:
Mixed summer greens
Fruit (berries, peaches)
Walnuts
Oil

Honey mustard seems to have many origins, from ancient Rome to French Arcadia. Used as a faith cure smeared across the chest by traiteurs, this dressing is bound to heal your hunger on summer nights when it's too hot too cook. You could have the salad ingredients raw, to avoid cooking altogether, but I've included cooking directions to better meld the flavors.

Combine dressing ingredients and process in food processor. Spray pan lightly with oil and wilt greens slightly on medium heat. Divide among plates. Add walnuts to pan and toast lightly. Divide among plates again. Top salads with berries and drizzle with dressing. For peaches, slice into 1/2" wedges and cook about 3 minutes per side. (You could also grill peaches and romaine leaves over foil pierced with holes.) Add to salads. Serve immediately.

Garden Dressing
Taste of Earth

Dressing:
2 tbs. olive oil
2 tbs. chive cider vinegar*
2 tbs. grated organic carrots
1 tsp. local honey
1 tsp. lemon juice
1/8 tsp. salt

Salad:
Mixed summer greens
Fresh tomatoes, cucumbers, zucchini, etc.
Grilled chicken or lamb (optional)
Grilled corn (optional)

This dressing comes straight from the garden and goes well with just about everything. Combine dressing ingredients and process in food processor until smooth. Drizzle over salads. Make as much as you need. Recipe can be easily multiplied, but is best served fresh. This recipe is good for 4-6 salads.

* Gather young chive blossoms, wash, and place them in a clean glass jar. Heat vinegar to simmering, then pour over blossoms. Let steep in vinegar several days, then strain out blossoms. Store in refridgerator.

Catalina Dressing
Taste of Spain

Dressing:
1 clove garlic, minced
2 tbs. cider vinegar
3 tbs. oil
2 tbs. local honey
1 cherry tomato (no need to cut)
1 tsp. mince onion
1 tsp. fresh chopped herb (tarragon, basil, or marjoram)

Salad Suggestion:
mixed summer greens
mixed sliced tomatoes
peeled sliced cucumber
fresh sliced mozzarella
pancetta, cooked (optional)

Catalina means "pure", as are the ingredients for this dressing inspired by Catalonia, Spain. Combine all dressing ingredients and process in food processor. Divide salad ingredients among plates. Drizzle with dressing. Serve immediately.

Other options: Use dressing as a marinade for chicken or fish. Mix into a seafood or pasta salad. Add to cole slaw or diced cucumbers for a zesty side dish.

Garlic Scape
Five Fast Fresh Fixes

White Bean and Garlic Scape Dip: In a food processor, blend 1/2 cup chopped garlic scape, 1 1/2 cups of drained cannellini beans (canned or soaked overnight), 2 tbs. grape seed oil, and 1 tbs. fresh finely-chopped dill. Salt and pepper to taste, but flavorful without them.

Scape Pesto: Chop scape and greens such as basil, parsley, oregano, or lemon balm in a food processor. Add nuts such as pine nuts, walnuts, or hazelnuts., processing until smooth. While processor is running, slowly pour in olive oil. Add lemon juice, if desired.

Scape Butter: Finely chop scape and stir into softened butter. Re-chill. Great for making garlic bread!

Scape Hummus: Add a tablespoon of minced scape to hummus recipe, page 145.

Tzatziki's Great E-Scape: Peel and seed one cucumber and grate. Mix with 2 cups of Greek yogurt, 1-2 tbs. minced scape, 2 tbs. lemon juice, 10 chopped mint leaves, and salt to taste. Chill at least one hour.

Parsley Sauce
Taste of Wales

1 1/2 tbs. salted butter or margarine
1 1/2 tbs. unbleached flour (use corn starch for gluten-free)
2-4 tbs. garlic scapes, chopped to 1/2" lengths (optional)
1 cup chopped parsley, packed
1/2 cup milk (or vegan substitute)
1/2 cup cream or half-and-half (or vegan substitute)
1/4 tsp. each salt and white pepper

Scape are the first sproutings of garlic, with curling tendrils and a milder taste. The sauce is good without them, but don't pass them up if they're around, June through July. You could also substitute diced garlic cloves. Process scape and parsley with milk in a food processor until uniform. In a medium sauce pan, melt butter over medium-low heat. Whisk in flour, stirring rapidly until thickened to a roux, about one minute. Slowly pour in cream, stirring frequently. Cook 5 minutes. Add parsley/scape mix, salt, and white pepper, stirring well. Cook another 5 minutes, then remove from heat. Use as a dip or sauce.

Tomato Sauce
Taste of Italy

Prep: 20 minutes Cook: 1 hour 15 minutes Makes 3 quarts

1 cup olive oil
1 large onion, chopped
3 garlic cloves, minced
1/2 cup minced fresh Italian parsley
10 leaves fresh basil, minced
1 tsp. oregano
1/2 tsp. thyme
1 tsp. salt
1/2 tsp. white pepper
1 cup dry red wine (merlot, sirah, shiraz)
1/4 cup tomato paste
2 cups reduced sodium vegetable or chicken broth
10 cups blanched and cored Roma tomatoes (about 8
    pounds or 50 tomatoes. Or use two 35 oz. cans of
    whole tomatoes)

In heavy saucepan, heat oil. Sauté onion and garlic over low heat five minutes. Add herbs, salt, pepper, tomato paste, and wine. Simmer 15 minutes or until onions are soft, stirring occasionally. Stir in broth and cook 10 more minutes, stirring often to prevent sticking. Add tomatoes, breaking up with spoon and blending well. Simmer uncovered 45 minutes, stirring occasionally. Cool completely before refrigerating or freezing. Recipe is not designed for canning.

Zippy Zucchini
Taste of Italy

1 cup washed, grated zucchini
1/2 cup grated carrot
2 tbs. butter
4 eggs, beaten
1/2 cup Narragansett Creamery Atwell's Gold, Parmesan or
   Asiago cheese
1/2 cup unbleached flour
1 tbs. fresh, chopped dill, marjoram, or thyme
1/4 tsp. salt
1/8 tsp. white pepper

This is a baked version of the famous zucchini fritters. Preheat oven to 350°F and grease a 12-count muffin tin. Melt butter and sauté zucchini and carrots until softened, about three minutes. Beat eggs in medium bowl, then whisk in vegetables, flour, cheese, herbs, salt, and pepper. Pour mixture into muffin tin, about 3/4 full. Bake 20-25 minutes, until toothpick comes out clean.

Recipe can also be cooked in a baking pan and cut into squares. This recipe works even if you double the amount of vegetables, so have at it!

Baba Ganoush
Taste of Lebanon

Prep: 5 minutes Cook: 40-60 minutes Makes 1 cup

1 cup roasted eggplant
4 garlic cloves, minced
1 1/2 tbs. tahini
2 tbs. lemon juice
1 tbs. fresh minced parsley
1 tsp. curry
1/4 tsp. salt

Preheat oven to 375°F. Wash eggplant and cut in half length-wise. Brush cut sides with olive oil and place face down in baking dish. Pierce skin all over with fork. Cut top off head of garlic and brush with olive oil. Put in pan with eggplant. Roast both until aromatic and tender, 40-60 minutes, depending on size of eggplant. Scoop out one cup of eggplant flesh when cool and combine with other ingredients in food processor. Recipe can be multiplied to accommodate available ingredients or extra garlic can be spread on toast and eggplant can be added to pizzas or calzones.

Mock-A-Mole
Taste of Mexico

2 cups fresh or thawed peas
1 clove garlic, diced
10 cherry tomatoes
1/2 jalapeño, seeded and diced
1/2 tsp. salt
1/2 tsp. cumin
1 tbs. olive oil
cilantro (optional)

I love avocados, which have many health benefits including Omega-3s and potassium. But in keeping with local food, this version has less fat, more calcium, iron, magnesium, phosphorus, protein, vitamins A and C, and zinc, and close to the same amount of folate as avocados. I realize olive oil is not local, but who doesn't have it in their pantry? Plus, it adds Omega-3s that otherwise would have come from the avocado. Combine all ingredients in a food processor and blend until smooth. Add more olive oil for smoother consistency. I made the cilantro optional because cilantro has usually gone to seed by late summer.

Fiesta Muffins
Taste of Mexico

Prep: 10 minutes Bake: 20-25 minutes Makes 24 muffins

1 1/2 cups unbleached flour
1 cup wheat flour
3 tsp. baking powder
1/4 tsp. baking soda
1 tsp. salt
1 tbs. dried oregano
2 eggs
1 cup homemade or good-quality salsa
1 cup of washed and shredded zucchini, summer
   squash, or spaghetti squash*
1/2 cup oil
1/2 cup shredded cheddar or Mexican cheese*

A savory choice for breakfast, parties, or a side dish, and by far my most popular potluck food. It's also a great way to sneak veggies into your kids! Preheat oven to 375°F. Sift dry ingredients. In separate bowl, mix wet. Add wet to dry. Grease two muffin trays and fill cups 3/4 full. Bake 25 minutes or until toothpick comes out clean. Yield: 24 muffins.

*Shred local squash and cheese on the same box grater.

Summery Succotash
Taste of Native America

Serves 4.

1 cup fresh sweet corn kernels (about 2 ears)
1/2 cup fresh lima and/or cranberry beans
1/4 cup red bell pepper, diced fine
1 tbs. butter or bacon fat (vegetable spread for vegan)
1 tsp. maple syrup
1/8 tsp. each salt and white pepper
2 slices bacon, well-cooked and crumbled (optional)

Succotash owes its name to the Narragansett tribe's word for it: msíckquatash. It consists of boiled corn kernels and beans and has many variations. Maize, as it's also called, originated from a grass in Mexico. After 10,000 years of cultivation, the large kernels we are all familiar with developed, carried northward from tribe to tribe. Lima beans are actually native to South America, with cranberry beans native to the Northeast. This succotash version gets added sweetness from red peppers and omits the European addition of cream. Serve it in a mini pumpkin and it's truly a "three sisters" meal.

In a large pot, bring water to a boil. Add husked corn cobs and shelled beans and cook until tender, about 20 minutes. Transfer corn to a bowl of ice water to cool. Retrieve beans with a slotted spoon. Dice pepper and cook bacon. Cut kernels from cooled cobs. Melt butter or bacon fat in sauté pan. Add all remaining ingredients and sauté on medium heat until vegetables start to glaze and crisp. Serve immediately.

Turnip
Four Fresh Fixes

Turnip Slaw: Grate 1/2 turnip with one head of cabbage. Mix with 1/2 cup apple cider vinegar, one tbs. sugar, one tbs. caraway seed, and 1/2 tsp. each salt and pepper. Chill overnight.

Turnips and Carrots: Peel and cut half a large turnip and 6 carrots into 1" pieces. Boil until tender, 10-15 minutes. Reserve liquid for stock. Stir in 2 tbs. butter and one tsp. of fresh chopped tarragon.

Turnip Stock: Peel and chop turnips. Cover with water in sauce pan and bring to boil. Cook until tender. Remove pieces from water and save for turnip nutmeg mash. Cool remaining liquid and freeze in ice cube trays. Store cubes in freezer bag and use for stock.

Macomber Turnip Nutmeg Mash: Peel and cut turnips. Boil turnips until tender. Remove from water (reserving liquid for stock) and mash with butter and fresh ground nutmeg.

Cabbage Cole Slaw
Taste of Holland

1/2 cabbage, shredded
1 bunch white radish, grated
1/2 diced red pepper or 1 grated carrot
1 tbs. white sugar
1 tbs. oil
1/4 cup cider vinegar
1 tbs. minced tarragon or oregano
Spice it up: Add red pepper flakes or diced jalapeño

When life gives you cabbage on a hot summer day, make "koosla", the shredded Dutch salad dish. Prepare vegetables. Heat sugar, oil, and vinegar to blend. Toss with vegetables and herbs. Chill at least one hour.

Fall/Winter variation: Add 1 cup cranberries that have been cooked over medium heat until just soft and popping, in just enough water to keep them from sticking to pan.

Coconut Cauliflower
Taste of the Caribbean

Prep: 15 minutes Cook: 20 minutes Serves 4

1 head of cauliflower, broken into bite-sized pieces
1/2 cup corn meal
1/4 cup unbleached flour* or gluten-free all-purpose flour
1/2 tsp. baking soda
1 egg
1 cup French vanilla yogurt (such as Stonyfield)
1 cup shredded coconut
1 tsp. almond extract
oil for frying

Taste Aruba with this twist on the classic coconut shrimp recipe. Whisk together dry ingredients. In a separate bowl, mix wet ingredients and coconut. Stir dry ingredients into wet. Let sit at least ten minutes to activate baking soda. Meanwhile, steam cauliflower covered in vegetable steamer basket until tender, about 5 minutes after water begins to boil. Cool and dry inside a clean towel. Heat two inches of oil to 160°F, or medium-high. Dip cauliflower pieces in batter and cook in oil in small batches, 30-45 seconds*, turning once during cooking time. Drain on cooling rack over baking tray. Serve as an appetizer with yogurt dipping sauce.

* wheat flour will take longer to cook

Clam Cakes

Taste of Rhode Island

Prep: 10 minutes Cook: 10-15 minutes Makes 40 cakes

1 egg
1 cup chopped quahog (or clams)
1/4 cup grated carrots
1/2 cup milk
1 1/2 cups corn meal
2 tsp. baking powder
1/2 tsp. salt
1/4 tsp. cayenne pepper
1 tsp. dried oregano
1 tsp. garlic powder
oil for frying

What would summer be without Rhode Island clam cakes? Rather than a heavy, doughy blob, these cook up light and don't skimp on the seafood. The carrots add to the sweetness of the seafood. Steam open quahogs, cool in cold water, and chop. Beat egg, then add all other ingredients. Heat about 2" of cooking oil in a sauce pan on high.* When oil sizzles when batter is added, drop one tbs. of batter at a time until a single layer of cakes floats on oil. Cook one minute, then remove with slotted spoon to paper towels or cooling rack over baking tray.

* I fry cakes in my smallest sauce pan to reduce the amount of oil needed. In my pan, I can cook five cakes at a time. After oil cools, it can be strained and kept in the refrigerator for future use.

Birth of Venus Soup
Taste of Greece

5 cups reduced-sodium chicken broth
4 eggs
5 tbs. lemon juice
1/3 cup rice
1/2 tsp. salt
1/4 tsp. white pepper
1-2 lbs. seafood such as local clams, littlenecks, or quahogs,
    and/or local butterfish, cod, or haddock, and/or scallops*
parsley for garnish

Botticelli brought us "The Birth of Venus", the goddess of love born full-grown on a clam shell (Aphrodite to the Greeks). If you love seafood, you'll love this soup. Bring broth to boil. Add rice and reduce to simmer, 20 minutes or until rice is cooked. In a separate pot, place any shelled seafood and cover with water. Bring water to a boil and cook just until shells open, about 3-5 minutes. Remove shellfish from shell and set aside. Whisk together eggs and lemon juice in bowl. Slowly whisk in about a cup of hot broth to eggs. Add this to the soup. Add fish or scallops and cook just until seafood becomes opaque, about three minutes. Add shellfish. Season with salt and pepper. Garnish with chopped parsley. Serve immediately.

* Three quahogs are about one pound. Keep shellfish in water until ready to use.

Kale Soup
Taste of Portugal

2 tbs. olive oil
6 cloves of garlic, coarsely chopped
2 medium onions, diced
4 Yukon Gold potatoes with skin, cut into 1/2" cubes
3 carrots, peeled and sliced 1/2" thick
1 turnip, peeled and cut into 1/2" cubes (optional)
1 large bunch of kale, minced
1 tbs. fresh stemmed lemon thyme (or 1 tsp. dried)
1 tsp. turmeric
1/2 tsp. each salt and white pepper
10 cups of stock (such as from boiled vegetables or chicken)
1 lb. chorizo, bacon, or vegan alternative

Heat oil in large stock pot. Sauté garlic and onions until translucent. Pour in stock and bring to boil. Add vegetables, herbs, and seasoning and return to boil. Reduce heat, and simmer 20 minutes, or until root vegetables are soft. While soup is simmering, fully cook meat(s): Slice and fry chorizo, microwave bacon well, or cook meat alternative according to package directions. Drain fat. For bacon, break into pieces. Add to cooked soup.

Main Dishes

Lamb Wraps

Scape Goat

Broccoli Bounty

Pansotti with Walnut Sauce

Cacciatore Catch-All

Coconut Curry

Chicken Mole Empanadas

Chicken Piccata

Rainbow Steak

You Say Mussaka

Ratatouille

Chicken and Peaches

Lamb Wraps
Taste of Greece

Prep: 15 minutes Chill: 1 hour Cook: 10 minutes Serves 6

1 cucumber, peeled, seeded, and grated
2 tsp. minced garlic or scapes, divided
2 tbs. minced fresh mint, divided
1 cup Greek yogurt
1 tbs. lemon juice
1/8 tsp. salt
1 tbs. minced fresh "Hot and Spicy" or Greek oregano
1/4 cup minced green onions or scallions
1 lb. ground lamb or pork
pita, lavash, or gluten-free wrap

Squeeze liquid from cucumber. Mix with yogurt, 1 tbs. mint and 1 tsp. garlic scapes, lemon juice, and salt and run through food processor. Chill at least one hour. Heat oil in sauté pan over medium heat. Add remaining mint and garlic scapes, oregano, and scallions or onions. Cook about 2 minutes, stirring constantly. Cool. Mix with lamb and form 1" meatballs. Cook in pan, turning every 2-3 minutes until brown on all sides and cooked through, 7-10 minutes. Serve meatballs in pita, lavash, or wrap with tzatziki yogurt sauce.

Scape Goat
Taste of Greece

2 lbs. young goat or lamb shanks, cut up
1/2 cup garlic scapes, chopped to 1/2" lengths
1/2 cup fresh stemmed and chopped "Hot and Spicy" or
   Greek oregano
1/4 cup fresh stemmed and chopped lemon thyme
1 tbs. grape seed or olive oil
2 cups of peeled carrots cut diagonally, 1/2" thick
3 potatoes with skin, scrubbed and sliced 1/2" thick
1 cup chopped celery or celeriac
1 large onion, roughly chopped
1/2 tsp. each salt and white pepper
3 tbs. tomato paste
1 cup dry red wine

Preheat oven to 350°F. Stem herbs by pulling leaves downward, discarding any discolored or dead leaves. Trim excess fat from meat. Heat oil in large stainless steel pan or Dutch oven on medium-high. Brown meat but do not cook through, about 3 minutes per side. Set meat aside and sprinkle with salt and pepper. Add carrots, potatoes, celery/celeriac, onion, and tomato paste and stir well. Cook about five minutes, or until onions soften. Add garlic scapes and cook 2-3 minutes more. Return meat to pan, pour in wine, and spread herbs over all. Heat to simmering. Cover pan with tight-fitting lid or foil and finish cooking in oven until meat is tender and falling off bone, about 1 1/2 to 2 hours. Serves 4.

Broccoli Bounty
Taste of America's South

Prep: 15 minutes Cook: 50-60 minutes Serves 6

4 cups fresh or frozen broccoli pieces, steamed
4 cups cooked rice or pasta
2 cups shredded cheese (local cheddar or Cabot's)
2 tbs. unsalted butter, divided
1 tbs. flour
1 cup reduced fat/low sodium chicken or vegetable broth
1 cup 1% local milk
1 tsp. each paprika and Bell's Seasoning,
1/2 tsp. each salt and pepper
1/4 cup Panko flakes

This can be made in late summer with fresh broccoli or anytime with blanched and frozen broccoli. This dish is high in calcium, both from the dairy and broccoli, and a hit with kids. Steam broccoli until tender and cook rice or pasta. Melt 1 tbs. butter in sauce pan over medium heat. Whisk in flour and stir continuously one minute. Slowly pour in broth and milk, along with seasonings. Stir in broccoli, rice or pasta, and cheese, mixing well. Transfer to casserole dish. Sprinkle with Panko flakes and dot with remainder of butter. Bake at 350°F for 30 minutes, until bubbly and golden.

Pansotti with Walnut Sauce
Taste of Italy

Prep: 1 hour Cook: 15 minutes Serves 10

Dough:
2 eggs
3/4 cup milk
1 tsp. cider vinegar
1 tsp. salt
2 3/4 cup unbleached flour

Filling:
1/4 cup blanched, towel-dried, minced borage or nettles*
1 cup ricotta (cow or goat)
1/4 cup dry white wine
1 tbs. chopped fresh basil*

Walnut Sauce:
1 shallot, minced
1 tbs. butter
1 cup chopped, toasted walnuts
1 cup whipping cream
1/4 tsp. liquid smoke

This dish takes time to make, but it well worth it. Serve it at a dinner party and enjoy the praise for making your own ravioli and rich sauce. Borage has a light cucumber taste and the hairy texture of the leaves disappears when you blanche them. For dough, whisk eggs, milk, and vinegar. Stir in salt and flour, then knead on heavily floured counter into a stretchy dough. Keep wrapped in plastic in refrigerator until needed later.

For filling, pick 25-30 borage leaves, carefully washing them and removing discolored parts. Boil leaves about 5 minutes to soften hairs, place in ice water 1 minute, then squeeze out excess water by placing leaves in a towel and pressing. Mince leaves on a cutting board, to yield a 1/4 cup. Mix thoroughly with cheese, wine, and basil. To make ravioli, roll dough out as thin as possible (the last setting on a pasta machine) and cut into 3" squares. Make sure area is heavily floured, as dough can get sticky. Place about 2 tsp. of filling on each square and fold over into a triangle. Separate ravioli on floured wax paper until ready to cook.

For sauce, toast walnuts gently in pan then set aside. Mince shallot and sauté in butter until just soft. Run nuts through food processor with some of cream to create a paste, leaving some pieces unprocessed if desired. Return nut mixture to pan with remaining cream. Heat gently, stirring in liquid smoke towards end.

Cook ravioli in boiling water 3-5 minutes. Drain and top with sauce. Use fresh basil leaves as garnish, if desired.

* Recipe also works with stinging nettles and/or lemon balm

Cacciatore Catch-All
Taste of Italy

Prep: 15 minutes Cook: 45 minutes Serves 4

2 lbs. local chicken parts (optional)
2 tbs. olive oil
1/2 red onion, diced
1 red or green bell pepper, coarsely chopped
4 cloves garlic, minced
2 cups peeled tomatoes* (Roma and/or cherry)
2 cups sliced chicken mushrooms** (or white button)
1 cup of "catch-all": washed and chopped zucchini, summer
    squash, eggplant, or what-have-you
1 tbs. dried oregano (or 2 tbs. fresh)
1/2 tsp. salt
1/4 tsp. white pepper
1/2 cup red wine (from freezer cubes?)

"Cacciatore" means hunter in Italian and often features wild mushrooms** (assuming the hunter did not want to come home empty-handed). This recipe is a great way to use up odds and ends from canning. Consider measurement of vegetables approximate. Leftovers can even be added to an omelet, frittata, or soup.

Heat olive oil on medium-high in Dutch oven or large skillet with cover. If using chicken, brown meat five minutes each side and set aside. Add onions, garlic, and bell pepper to pan. Cook two minutes, or until onions

soften. Add tomatoes, mushrooms, and remaining vegetables. Season with salt, pepper, and oregano. Add
wine and bring to boil. Reduce heat to simmer. Add
chicken and cover. Cook 30 minutes, or until chick-
en reaches 165°F and vegetables are soft. Serve with
crusty bread, pasta, or rice.

* When canning tomatoes, skins are removed by blanching. This is
done by dropping whole tomatoes in boiling water about one minute,
then into ice water one minute, to easily peel skin. I've used the leftover
seeds and juice from canning harissa sauce with plum tomatoes. You
could also use already canned tomatoes or just chop fresh tomatoes and
leave skins on.

** Do not attempt to gather wild mushrooms without a certified guide.
Chicken and Hen of the Woods are the easiest to recognize. Puffballs
(Calvatia gigantea) should be the size of two fists or larger and white
throughout. Discolored puffballs are not safe to eat and will not taste
good. Immature amanita can be mistaken for puffballs, thus the need
to look for larger mushrooms. (Puffballs can grow quite large and have
even been mistaken for Styrofoam trash in littered woodlands!) Cutting
the mushroom may reveal more: A "U" shape indicates the immature
cap of the poisonous amanita, but may not always be visible. Alcohol
intensifies reaction to any poisonous mushroom. Don't risk it!!! The
author and publisher assume no liability for injury, poisoning, illness,
or death from consuming wild mushrooms or plants. Leave it to the
experts: Chicken, Hen of the Woods, and Puffballs may be available at
some farmers' markets or high-end food stores.

Coconut Curry
Taste of India

Prep: 20 minutes Cook: 30-35 minutes Makes 8 servings

2 tbs. oil, melted butter or ghee*
1/2 cauliflower, stemmed and broken into bite-sized pieces
2 medium potatoes, scrubbed and cut into 1/2" cubes
1/2 onion, roughly chopped
3 garlic cloves, minced
1 tsp. peeled, finely grated ginger root
1-2 jalapeños or other green chili, seeded and chopped
1 tbs. paprika
2 tsp. garam masala (Combine coriander, pepper, cumin,
    cardamom, and cinnamon. Also at stores.)
1 tsp. organic curry powder
1 cup reduced sodium vegetable or chicken broth
1/2 eggplant, cut into 1/2" cubes
1 1/2 cups blanched, cored, chopped tomatoes (any kind)
4 okra, sliced into 1/2" stars
1 tbs. corn starch
2/3 cup coconut milk
1/2 cup roasted, unsalted cashews

A true taste of India requires some ingredients from afar, but you'll find all the produce at Farmer's Markets by the end of summer. The creamy coconut sauce is thickened with cashews (which the Portuguese brought to India from Brazil). In a large sauté pan with lid, heat oil, butter, or ghee. Add onion, potato, and cauliflower, and cook over medium heat five minutes, stirring frequently.

Add garlic, ginger, and spices, stirring well and cooking one minute. Add stock, stirring up any bits from pan. Add eggplant and tomatoes, mixing well. Cover and cook 15 minutes, stirring occasionally. Add okra and cook 10-15 minutes more, or until tender. In blender, blend corn starch, coconut milk, and cashews until smooth. Stir into vegetable mixture, stirring constantly, about two minutes. Serve hot, with jasmine rice if desired.

* Ghee is butter that has been melted and the fat skimmed off when cool. It can be prepared ahead and stores well. It can also be purchased at Indian specialty shops, where you may find better prices for the curry and garam masala.

Chicken Mole Empanadas
Taste of Mexico

Prep: 20 minutes Chill: 1 hour Cook: 55 minutes Makes 24

Filling:
1-2 tbs. cooking oil
3/4 lb. chicken tenderloin
1 yellow onion, diced
1 red bell pepper, seeded, ribbed, and diced
2 carrots, peeled and grated
2 cloves garlic, minced
1 jalapeño, seeded and chopped
1 tsp. plus 1/4 tsp. cumin, divided
2 tbs. chili powder
1 tsp. cinnamon
1 tsp. salt
2 tbs. brown sugar
2 tsp. tomato paste
1 tsp. lime juice
2 oz. dark chocolate (such as Green & Black's 70% Dark)

Preheat oven to 375°F. Trim fat and tendons from meat. Place in baking dish, brush with oil, and sprinkle with 1 tsp. cumin. Pierce meat all over with fork. Bake 25 minutes. Cool in bowl placed in larger bowl with ice.

Heat 1 tbs. oil on med-high in a large sauté pan. Add onion, red bell pepper, and carrot, cooking five minutes. Add garlic, jalapeño, spices, and salt and cook three minutes. Stir in tomato paste and brown sugar. Cook two more minutes, adding water if mixture sticks. Remove from heat and stir in chocolate to melt. Shred chicken and stir into mix. Mix in lime juice and salt. Let cool.

Dough:
3 cups all-purpose flour or GF flour
1 cup corn meal
2 tbs. sugar
2 tsp. cinnamon
1 tsp. salt
1/2 cup unsalted butter or shortening
1 egg
app. 1 cup water

Whisk together dry ingredients. Cut in butter or shortening. In separate bowl, whisk together egg and 1/2 cup of water. Mix with rest of ingredients, adding more water until dough forms. Chill 1 hour.

Preheat oven to 400°F. Divide dough into 12 balls. Roll each ball into a 6″ circle. Place 1/4 cup of filling in center of each circle. Fold circle over and seal with water. Use a fork to make a decorative edge. Bake empanadas on ungreased cookie sheet at 400°F for 20 minutes. Serve hot.

Chicken Piccata
Taste of Italy

Prep: 10 minutes Cook: 20 minutes Serves 6

2 lbs. chicken tenders, tendons removed and fat trimmed
1/2 tsp. each salt and pepper
1/2 cup unbleached flour
2 tbs. butter, divided
2 tbs. olive oil, divided
1/2 cup chicken broth
1/4 cup dry white wine (such as Pinot Grigio)
1 tbs. fresh lemon balm leaves, minced
1 tbs. pickled nasturtium seeds* (or capers)
nasturtium leaves, for garnish (optional)

Place tenderloins on a cutting board and cover with two sheets of wax paper. Tap with rubber mallet to soften meat, until meat is 1/4" thick. Sprinkle with salt and pepper. Dredge in flour. Heat 1 tbs. each of butter and olive oil in large sauté pan over medium heat. Cook chicken three-quarters through before turning, about five minutes. Cook 2-3 minutes more. Set meat aside. Use remaining butter and olive oil to cook remaining chicken. Set meat aside. Add broth, wine, lemon balm, and nasturtium seeds or capers to pan. Bring to a gentle boil, scraping up brown bits, until slightly thickened. Return chicken and heat through. Serve with pasta. Garnish with nasturtium leaves, if desired.

* Nasturtium seeds can be pickled by soaking them in a mix of one cup water, one cup vinegar, and 3 tbs. canning salt in the refrigerator at least one week. If you are making pickles, use your leftover brine. Seeds will keep several months.

Rainbow Steak

Taste of Tex-Mex

Prep: 15 minutes Cook: 20 minutes Serves 4

1 lb. steak, cut diagonally into 1/2" strips
1 tbs. olive oil
2 tbs. Balsamic vinegar
1 tbs. cumin
1/8 tsp. each salt and pepper
2 cups chopped red, orange, yellow, and green bell peppers
1/2 red onion, diced
1/2 cup parsley, finely chopped
juice of half a lime (slice other half into wedges for garnish)

Marinate steak in vinegar at least 20 minutes, piercing meat all over with knife. Heat oil in sauté pan over med-high heat. Add steak, cooking 3-4 minutes per side. Remove meat and set aside. Add peppers and onions to same pan, cooking until tender-crisp. Add a little water or broth if vegetables start to stick. Remove from heat and stir in parsley, lime, salt, and pepper. Serve immediately with fiesta muffins (page 65) and baked potatoes or hot or cold over a bed of greens and fresh tomatoes, with a Balsamic dressing.

You Say Mussaka

Taste of the Mediterranean

Prep: 15 minutes Cook: 15-30 minutes Serves 6

1 medium eggplant, peeled and cut into 1/2" cubes
1 tbs. olive oil
2 tsp. fresh ground coriander
1 1/2 tbs. paprika
1 tsp. cumin
1/2 tsp. cinnamon
1/2 cup of onion (mix of green, yellow, or red, just avoid
    using tough stems)
4 cloves garlic, minced*
1 15 oz. can chickpeas, drained and rinsed (or 2 cups local
    beans, soaked overnight)
4 cups of zucchini, quartered lengthwise and sliced 1/2"
    thick, and/or summer squash mix, chopped
2 cups of heirloom tomatoes, roughly chopped (halve cherry
    tomatoes)
2 cups plus 1/4 cup vegetable or chicken broth
1 cup quinoa (gluten-free) or couscous
4 tbs. chopped nasturtium leaves and/or parsley
1 lb. ground lamb (optional)

Lebanon meets Tunisia in this mussaka/ragout-inspired
dish. Place eggplant cubes in a single layer on a baking
sheet and spray with olive oil. Bake at 475°F 15 minutes, stirring halfway through baking time. Meanwhile,
heat olive oil in large sauté pan. Heat spices one minute. If using meat, brown meat in same pan, then set

aside. Add garlic and onions to pan, starting with more oil if necessary. Cook two more minutes. Add chick peas and cook until lightly toasted, coating in spices and onion/garlic blend. Add zucchini and/or squash and 1/4 cup of broth, mixing well. Bring to boil then reduce to simmer. Add eggplant (and meat, if using) and simmer, covered, 10-15 minutes. While that simmers, prepare couscous or quinoa. For quinoa, rinse one cup of dry grains. Heat small sauce pan, then toast grains until they're almost dry. Add two cups of broth, bring to boil, then reduce heat and cover. Cook until all liquid is absorbed, about 15 minutes. Stir chopped tomatoes and nasturtium leaves or parsley into vegetable mix. Divide couscous or quinoa among plates and top with mussaka/ragout mixture. Sprinkle generously with fresh chopped nasturtium leaves and/or parsley.

* If using fresh garlic, use a micro-planer to tear an opening to help you peel it. Use a fork or corn skewer to hold clove as you mince it.

Ratatouille

Taste of Mediterranean France

Prep: 10 minutes Cook: 30 minutes Makes 8 servings

4 cloves of garlic, thinly sliced width-wise
1 tbs. double-concentrated tomato paste
2 tbs. olive oil, divided
1/2 yellow onion*
1 medium Italian eggplant (I love Rotonda Bianca Sfumata
    di Rosa, an heirloom variety with few seeds)*
5 Roma tomatoes*
4 cups mixed summer squash (crook- and straight-neck,
    patty pan or scalloped, zucchini, etc.)*
1/2 cup grated Parmesan cheese (optional)
1 tbs. fresh stemmed and finely chopped lemon thyme
1/2 tsp. salt
1/4 tsp. white pepper

This dish cooks up fast with the aid of a mandoline. Pre-heat oven to 375°F. Slice onion, eggplant, tomatoes, and squash 1/4" thin, keeping each vegetable separate. There is no need to salt the eggplant first or even peel it. Cutting the vegetables this way is fast, attractive, and saves on cooking time. In a covered skillet or Dutch oven, heat one tbs. olive oil. Sauté garlic one minute, stirring frequently. Add onions and tomato paste, stir-ring well. Cook until onions wilt, about five minutes. Add eggplant and tomatoes, cover, and cook 10 min-utes, stirring occasionally and adding water if necessary to prevent sticking. Stir in herbs, salt, and pepper. Sprinkle with cheese. Layer with squash and drizzle with another tablespoon of olive oil. Cover and cook at 375°F 10-15 minutes, until squash are soft. Serve by carefully spooning onto plates to retain layers. Great with pasta or warm crusty bread. Use leftovers in a frittata or on a pizza. Tastes even better reheated.

* Cut flower end from vegetables and hold stem while slicing on mandoline. Mandoline blades are very sharp, so take care to keep fingers clear. Although many models are pricey, a 4-piece set can be found for less than $20. Use safety guard to slice onion on mandoline, or slice by hand.

Chicken and Peaches
Taste of Tunisia

2 tbs. oil, divided
2 cups diced red onion
1/2 cup sliced almonds
1 tsp. white pepper
1 tsp. cinnamon
2 lbs. boneless, skinless chicken thighs, fat trimmed
3 cups reduced fat, low sodium (gluten-free) chicken broth
2 organic peaches, cut into wedges then halved*
2 tbs. honey
1 pinch saffron (optional)
couscous (not gluten-free) or rice

This recipe is based on the sweet tangine dishes of North Africa, but has less sugar and fat than traditional recipes. By using boneless chicken thighs instead of whole chicken, it also cooks faster and costs less to prepare. In a covered skillet or Dutch oven, heat 1 tbs. of oil on medium-high. Cook onions, nuts, and spices, stirring frequently, about three minutes. Remove mixture and set aside. Add another tbs. of oil and brown thighs, about 2 minutes per side. Add stock and onion mixture and bring to a boil. Reduce heat slightly, cover, and poach gently 20 minutes. Uncover and add peaches, honey, and saffron, crushing spice with your fingers and sprinkling on top. Cook another 10-15 minutes, allowing liquid to thicken, until chicken flakes apart easily with a fork and meat thermometer reads 165°F.

Serve over couscous or use rice for gluten-free option.

* In other seasons, use peaches canned from summer pickings, using a tested recipe such as "Honey Peaches" from <u>Ball Complete Book of Home Preserving</u>.

Treats

Peach "Gelato"
Indian Pudding and Peaches
Revenge of the Squash Squares
Rose Hip Butter
Blueberry Chambord Jam

Peach "Gelato"
Taste of Italy

Prep: 15 minutes Freeze: 1 hour or overnight Serves 4

2 over-ripe peaches
1/2 cup half-and-half
2 tbs. local honey
1 tsp. ground ginger

Have peaches getting soft on your counter? Make this quick dessert! Soft peaches are easy to peel the skin from. You can peel, then freeze, or vice-versa. I usually freeze the peaches in their skins so I don't have to wrap them, but peeling must be done quick so peaches don't thaw. Freeze peaches at least one hour, preferably overnight. Remove pit by slicing around peach and twisting sides. Chop pitted peaches and mix with half-and-half, honey, and ground ginger in a blender until smooth. Serve immediately.

Indian Pudding and Peaches
Taste of Colonial New England

Prep: 15 minutes Cook: 1 hour (45 minutes baking) Serves 6

2 1/2 cups low-fat milk
1/3 cup cornmeal
1/4 cup molasses
1/4 cup real maple syrup
2 tbs. butter
2 eggs
1/2 tsp. fresh ground nutmeg
1/4 tsp. cardamom
2 organic peaches (or other seasonal fruit of choice)
1 cup light cream or half-and-half

Contrary to the name, this dish is not Native American in origin aside from the cornmeal, which was more readily available to the pilgrims than wheat flour. It's also called "hasty pudding" and at least cooks faster than some 3 hour recipes I've seen. With the molasses from the sugar trade not coming from North America or Europe, this dish was uniquely New England. I've added maple syrup to make it more "native", but couldn't resist Indonesian nutmeg and Asian Indian cardamom (a relative of ginger).

Preheat oven to 300°F and grease casserole dish. Pour milk into large sauce pan and heat on med-high until scalded but not boiling. (Look for tiny bubbles around the edges of the pot.) Whisk in the corn meal a table-spoon at a time, stirring well to prevent lumps. Add molasses, syrup, and butter. Reduce heat and cook 10-15 minutes, stirring frequently, until the consistency of pourable porridge. In a separate bowl, whisk eggs and spices together. Slowly add cornmeal mix to eggs, whisking constantly so as not to cook eggs. Pour mix into casserole dish and bake 45 minutes. Wash, pit, and cut peaches into half-wedges, or bite-sized pieces, leaving skin on. Serve pudding warm with peaches and a drizzle of cream or half-and-half.

Revenge of the Squash Squares
Taste of Earth

Prep: 15 minutes Bake: 30-35 minutes Makes 35 squares

2 cups unbleached flour
2 tbs. baking chocolate (preferably organic/free-trade)
1 tsp. baking soda
1 tsp. baking powder
1 tsp. ground coriander
1/2 tsp. cinnamon
1 egg
1/2 cup vegetable oil
1/2 cup plain or vanilla yogurt
3/4 cup white sugar
1 tsp. vanilla extract (if using plain yogurt)
1 cup grated summer squash or zucchini
1/2 cup mini chocolate chips
1/3 cup chopped walnuts (optional)

Are the squash taking over? Take revenge by baking them into moist, chocolate squares that will quickly disappear. Preheat oven to 325°F. In medium bowl, sift dry ingredients. In large bowl, whisk together egg and oil. Whisk in yogurt, sugar, and vanilla to egg mixture. Fold in squash, chips, and nuts, if using, then gradually stir in flour mixture. Bake in greased 9"X13" pan 30-35 minutes at 325°F. Cut into 35 squares (five down, seven across). Serve warm or cold, with ice cream if desired.

Rose Hip Butter
Taste of Earth

Prep: 20 minutes Cook: 10 minutes Makes 2 cups

1 1/2 cups rose hips*
1 cup white sugar
1/2 cup water
2 tsp. lemon juice
1 tsp. cinnamon (optional)

Although called butter, it's really a thick spread and could be made with most tree fruit, such as apples and pears. When selecting rose hips, choose large, firm ones without blemishes. If you are rewilding, gather rose hips in late summer from an area far from road sides or where pesticides may have been used. Beach roses have the largest hips. Some are invasive species, so if you can't beat them, eat them! Wash hips carefully, discarding soft or discolored "fruit". Cut each hip in half, scoop out seeds, then separate flesh from skin. This step is labor-intensive, so put on some music or invite a friend to chat.

Combine rose hips and water in sauce pan. Gently boil until soft. Use immersion blender or food processor and blend until smooth. Return to pan, if needed, and add sugar, mixing well. Bring back to boil, then reduce to simmer, until mixture is thick. Stir in lemon juice and cinnamon, if desired. Use within a week. Wonderful on whole wheat toast, stuffed French toast, and ice cream.

Blueberry Chambord Jam
Taste of France

6 cups washed and stemmed blueberries
1/2 cup water
2 tbs. lemon juice
zest of one organic lemon*
7 cups sugar
2 pouches liquid pectin (such as Ball or Certo)
1/4 cup Chambord or black raspberry liqueur (one nip)

New England summers would not be the same without blueberries. This jam is punched up by the French raspberry liqueur and lemon zest. Combine berries, water, lemon juice, and zest in large sauté pan and let sit ten minutes. Add sugar and mix well, until sugar completely dissolves. Bring mixture to boil and boil hard one minute, stirring constantly and skimming off any foam. Remove from heat and stir in pectin and Chambord. Using a measuring cup, pour into sterilized pint jars, leaving 1/2″ head-space. Wipe rims if necessary and attach lids securely. Process in pressure canner according to manufacturer's instructions, for 10 minutes at 10 psi. Makes 9 pints. (Process 8 and keep one in fridge.)

* While most citrus is in season during the cooler New England months, lemons are in season year-round. If you juice a lemon and don't need the zest right away, you can keep it in a bag in the freezer.

Try these in the winter, or any time:

1. Mix blueberry preserves with ricotta or other soft
   cheese (such as yogurt cheese, page 173). Use as
   spread or crêpe filling.
2. Warm preserves and spoon over ice cream.
3. Mix with yogurt.
4. Spread on toast.
5. Serve with pork.

Leaves change hue and flowers set seed. The earth prepares for rest, to become tomb and womb as acorns get buried by squirrels and fallen fruits resurrect in the spring from their protective seeds. The bounty is celebrated in a number of festivals. Pumpkins are eaten and carved. Apples transform into sauce and pies if they aren't eaten outright. Winter squash and roots are stored, perhaps apples as well. The garden is put to bed too. What's in Season: Apples • Arugula • Beets • Bok Choy • Broccoli • Brussels Sprouts • Cabbage • Carrots • Callaloo • Cardoon • Cauliflower • Celeriac • Chard • Cider • Collards • Corn • Cucumbers • Dried Fruit • Frozen Fruit • Frozen Vegetables • Garlic • Granola • Honey • Kale • Leeks • Maple Syrup • Microgreens • Mushrooms (fresh and dried): Crimini, Oyster, Portabella • Nuts • Onions • Parsnips • Peaches • Potatoes • Potted Herbs • Salad Greens • Shallots • Sprouts • Sweet Potatoes • Turnips • Winter Squash • Dairy:

AUTUMN

Cheese (cow, goat) • Eggs (chicken, duck, goose) • Milk (cow, goat) • Yogurt (cow, goat) • Meat: Beef • Chicken • Duck • Fowl • Goat • Lamb • Pork • Turkey • Seafood: Butterfish • Cod • Crab • Flounder • Haddock • Littleneck Clams • Lobster • Mackerel • Monkfish • Mussels • Oysters • Pollock • Quahogs • Scallops • Sea Bass • Sea Robins • Seaweed • Shrimp • Skate Wings • Squid • Steamers • Striped Bass • Swordfish • Tuna Wild Foods: Hen of the Woods, Chicken of the Woods, Acorns What to Do: Find Street and Harvest Festivals • Can Your Harvest • Store Root and Winter Vegetables • Go Gnome-Hunting: Photograph Mushrooms! • Pick Apples, Cherries, Peaches, Pawpaws, and Pears • Harvest Acorns • Make Corn Dollies • Make a Bittersweet Wreath • Fly a Kite • Plant Bulbs • Visit Haunted Sites • Make a Grave Rubbing • Build a Fairy House with Sticks, Acorns, Leaves, Pine Cones, Moss, Etc. • Carve Pumpkins and Radish with Faces, Scenes, Constellations, and Words

Salads, Sides, and Soups

Turnips for Two
Hungary for Sprouts
Firecracker Rolls
Pumpkin Polenta
Autumn Quinoa
Autumn Medley
Sweet Potato Samosa
Apple Parsnip Soup
Corn and Bean Chowder
Mushroom Fennel Soup
Borscht

Turnips for Two
Taste of France

Prep: 5 minutes Cook: 25 minutes Makes 2 servings

3 cups Milan turnips, peeled and sliced thin
1 tbs. butter
1 tsp. ground ginger
2 tsp. brown sugar
1/2 tsp. salt
splash of (hard) cider

Boil turnips gently in just enough water to cover until tender, about ten minutes. Melt butter in a sauté pan or cast iron skillet over medium heat. Stir in ginger and sugar until well-combined. Add drained turnips and stir well to coat. Cook over med-low heat 10-15 minutes. When turnips are aromatic, soft, and starting to crisp at edges, add a splash of cider and cook off, 1-2 minutes. Serve immediately.

Hungary for Sprouts!
Taste of Germany/Hungary

1 pt. Brussels sprouts
1 carrot
1/2 yellow onion
1 cup broth (vegetable, chicken, or beef)
1/4 tsp. each salt, white pepper, lemon thyme
1 tsp. brown mustard
protein: 4 sausage links, or 10 slices of bacon, or 1 1/2 cups
  of textured vegetable protein
oil for cooking

Wash Brussels sprouts, picking off yellow or discolored leaves. Halve each and slice halves thinly. Peel and grate carrot. Set both aside. Compost scraps. Heat oil in large sauté pan over medium heat. Open up sausage links, if using, and cook meat through. Or cook bacon on stove, using a tablespoon of the fat to start onions. Or cook vegetable protein until hot. Set meat aside. Dice onion and sauté in same pan 3-5 minutes, until translucent. Add sprouts and carrots and cook 1-2 minutes, stirring well. Pour in broth and add spices and mustard, stirring well. Cook 10-15 minutes, testing sprouts for sweetness and cooking until just soft. Serve with oven-roasted potatoes. This makes a great side dish at Thanksgiving!

Pumpkin Polenta
Taste of Italy

Prep: 10 minutes Cook: 15 minutes Makes 12 half-cup servings

1 tbs. olive oil
1 medium onion, diced
1 tbs. Balsamic vinegar (use cider vinegar for sulfite
  allergies)
2 tbs. finely cut fresh sage (or 1 tbs. dried), divided
2 cups baked pumpkin (or one 15 oz. can)
1 cup reduced sodium chicken or vegetable broth
32 oz. box of pre-cooked polenta, cut into 1/2" cubes
  (about 5 cups)*

Create layers of flavor in this quick side dish, perfect as a gluten-free stuffing for Thanksgiving! Heat oil over medium heat in a large sauté pan. Add diced onions and cook five minutes, stirring frequently. Add balsamic vinegar, stirring well, and cook three minutes. Stir in 1 tbs. of sage and cook another two minutes. Add remaining sage, pumpkin, polenta, and broth, mixing well. Simmer gently, stirring occasionally, until moisture is absorbed and onions are soft – about five minutes. Serve as a side dish or use as stuffing. This dish reheats well!

* If using uncooked polenta, follow package directions and chill before cutting into cubes.

Firecracker Cabbage Rolls
Taste of China

Prep: 20 minutes Cook: 20 minutes Makes: 20-40

1 tbs. olive oil
1 cup chopped, re-hydrated Asian mushrooms, or oyster and/or
  shiitake mushrooms (Wild: Chicken or Hen of the Woods*)
1/2 pound ground turkey or pork (optional)
2 cups grated cabbage
1 cup grated organic carrots
1/4 cup diced onion
1 tbs. minced fennel leaf (or 1 tsp. fennel seed)
20 sheets thawed phyllo dough
coconut oil spray

Chili Paste**:
2 Anaheim chiles, re-hydrated and chopped
1 tbs. cider vinegar
1 tbs. chile water
1 tsp. white sugar
1/8 tsp. salt
2 cloves garlic, chopped

Preheat oven to 375°F. Heat oil in large sauté pan or
Dutch oven over medium heat. Brown meat, if using.
Add mushrooms*, cabbage, carrots, onion, and fennel,
cooking until vegetable are tender, 5-7 minutes. Remove
from heat. Run chile mixture** through food processor
and stir into cabbage mix.

Cut phyllo sheets in half across the width. Place 2 tbs. cabbage mix along end of sheet and roll 4-5 layers tightly to other end. Spray baking sheet with coconut oil. Place each roll on baking sheet and spray rolls again. (Coconut oil will make rolls crispy without adding fat and calories that brushed oil or frying would.) Bake at 375°F 18-20 minutes, until golden. After cooling five minutes, rolls can be cut into smaller portions.

* Always cook wild mushrooms thoroughly. Do not attempt to gather wild mushrooms without a certified guide. The author and publisher assume no liability for injury, poisoning, illness, or death from consuming wild mushrooms or plants. Leave it to the experts: Wild mushrooms may be available at some farmers' markets or high-end food stores.

** In a hurry? Use Sriracha sauce in place of chili paste.

Autumn Quinoa
Taste of Earth

3/4 cup autumn olives or cranberries
1 cup red quinoa
2 cups chicken or vegetable broth
1/2 medium onion, diced
1/2 cup toasted almonds, flax or pumpkin seed, or combination
3 tbs. chopped fresh parsley
1 tbs. olive oil
1 tbs. Balsamic vinegar (use cider vinegar for sulfite
  allergies)

Autumn olives, or beginga berries, are native to Asia. Nitrogen-fixing, but invasive, they've been used to colonize disturbed soil for farmers. They are banned in several states because of their invasiveness, but with 17 times the lycopene of a tomato and mostly found in places where not much else will grow, why knock a free food source? They can be substituted for cranberries, but because of their mildly chewy edible pith, they are not recommended for jams or chutneys.

Dice onion and sauté in olive oil over medium heat in sauce pan until translucent and slightly crisp. Add vinegar and simmer one minute. Add quinoa, nuts, and seeds, stirring well. Cook 2-3 minutes. Add broth and bring to boil. Cover and reduce heat to simmer 15-20 minutes, until quinoa is tender and broth is absorbed. Turn off heat and stir in berries and chopped parsley. Serve immediately.

Autumn Medley
Taste of Italy

Prep: 20 minutes Cook: 45 to 60 minutes Makes: 6 cups

4 cups peeled, organic winter squash cut into 1" cubes
    (acorn, buttercup, butternut, and/or turban squash)
2 cups Bosc or Comice pears, cut into 1" cubes with skin
2 tsp. Worcestershire sauce
6 sprigs fresh organic lemon thyme
1/4 cup chopped pecans
1/2 cup Gorgonzola Picante, crumbled (local, if available)

Preheat oven to 450°F. Place cubed squash and pear in glass baking dish and drizzle with Worcestershire sauce. Sprinkle on thyme. Stir gently to incorporate. Bake 40 or more minutes, until squash is soft. Meanwhile, lightly toast pecans in sauté pan or cast iron skillet, dry or with oil, stirring frequently until nuts release aroma. Remove squash and pear dish from oven and stir in nuts and crumbled Gorgonzola. Serve immediately.

Sweet Potato Samosas
Taste of India

Prep: 25 minutes Cook: 5 minutes Makes about 2 dozen

Dough:
2 cups all-purpose flour
1 tsp. salt
1/2 cup Greek yogurt
4 tbs. butter, melted
1 tsp. cinnamon
1/4 - 1/2 cup water

Filling:
1 large sweet potato
1 yellow onion, diced
1 large apple, peeled
 and diced 1/2"
2 tbs. butter
1 tsp. yellow curry
1 tsp. ground ginger

For dough, sift flour and salt. Stir in melted butter and yogurt. Starting with a 1/4 cup water, mix dough, adding a tbs. at a time until a stiff dough forms. On floured surface with floured hands, knead until elastic. Roll out to 1/4" and cut into 4" circles. Reroll scraps and repeat.

Pierce sweet potato all over with fork and microwave 3-5 minutes, until soft. Cut in half to allow quicker cooling. Melt butter for filling over medium heat in large skillet. Add onion, apple, and spices. Cook until golden, about 5 minutes, stirring occasionally. Scoop out sweet potato into skillet, using oven mitt if still hot. Mix thoroughly and remove from heat.

Fill circles with a tablespoon of filling and fold over, pressing seams firmly. Fry in small batches in 3" of hot oil, 30-45 seconds, removing to drain on cooling rack over tray.

Gluten-Free/Vegetarian Option

Apple Parsnip Soup
Taste of Ireland

Prep: 15 minutes Cook: 25 minutes Serves 8

3 cups parsnips, peeled and sliced 1/2" thick (about 1 lb.)
2 tbs. butter or oil
1/2 yellow onion, diced
1 carrot, grated
1/2 cup grated celeriac (extra can be stored in freezer)
5 cups no salt broth (chicken or vegetable)
1/2 tsp. each salt and pepper
1 tsp. dried crushed sage
3 whole cloves
4 cups green apples, peeled, cored, and cut into 1/2" cubes
1/2 cup or more plain yogurt, sour cream, or crème fraîche

Heat butter or oil over medium heat in large sauce pan. Add onion, carrots, celeriac, and parsnips, stirring occasionally, cooking five minutes. Meanwhile, prep apples so they will be fresh. Add salt, pepper, sage, and cloves, cooking until aromatic. Add apples and broth. Reduce heat to simmer until parsnips are soft, about 20 minutes. In small batches, pour soup into blender and blend until smooth, or use an immersion blender. Divide soup among bowls and stir into each one 2 tbs. of plain yogurt, sour cream, or crème fraîche, leaving a white swirl. Serve immediately.

Corn & Bean Chowder
Taste of New England

Prep: 15 minutes Cook: 35 minutes Makes 10 servings

2 tbs. butter or olive oil
1 onion, diced
1 tbs. whole wheat flour or corn starch
2 cups (gluten-free) chicken or vegetable broth
2 cups low-fat milk
4 potatoes, washed and diced with skins on
1 cup carrots, cut into half-moons
1 cup fresh cranberry beans (soak dried beans overnight)
3 cups fresh-cooked or frozen corn
10 sliced of bacon, cooked well and drained (optional)
3 tbs. chopped fresh parsley or cilantro
1/2 tsp. salt
1/4 tsp. cayenne
1 tsp. cumin
1 tbs. brown sugar
1 cup half-and-half or light cream

Melt butter or heat oil over medium heat in large stock pot. Sauté onions five minutes. Stir in flour, cooking two minutes. Slowly pour in broth and milk. Add potatoes and carrots and bring to boil. Reduce heat to simmer and cook 15 minutes, or until vegetables are tender. Meanwhile, bring water to boil in sauce pan. Cook cranberry beans until just soft, about 20-25 minutes. Reserve. Add corn and mix with immersion blender (or run half of mixture through blender and return to stock pot). Crumble in bacon, then stir in drained beans, herbs, spices, sugar, and cream. Serve immediately.

Mushroom Fennel Soup
Taste of Earth

Prep: 10 minutes Cook: 45 minutes Makes: 6 cups

1 tbs. butter or oil
1 cup fennel stalks and leaves (lovage also works well)
1 cup sliced fresh or re-hydrated mushrooms*
1/2 red onion, sliced
1 cup mushroom broth*
3 cups chicken or vegetable broth

Pour boiling water over dried mushrooms and let steep 10-15 minutes. Finely chop fennel and slice onion. Drain mushrooms, reserving one cup of liquid. Slice mushrooms. Melt butter or oil in sauce pan. Sauté fennel, mushrooms, and onions until onions are tender, about ten minutes. Add broth and bring to boil. Reduce heat to low and simmer un-covered 30-35 minutes, until broth is rich and mushrooms plump. Serve with garlic bread, if desired.

* Shitake, oyster, or crimini mushrooms can be found dried at specialty food stores. Wild Option: Chicken mushrooms or Hen of the Woods. Always cook wild mushrooms thoroughly. Always be sure of mushroom identification before eating. Do not attempt to gather wild mushrooms without a certified guide. The author and publisher assume no liability for injury, poisoning, illness, or death from consuming wild mushrooms or plants. Leave it to the experts: Wild mushrooms may be available at some farmers' markets or high-end food stores

Borscht

Taste of the Ukraine

Prep: 10 minutes Cook: 25 minutes Serves: 6

1 onion, sliced thin
2 cups thinly sliced red cabbage
4 tbs. olive oil
2 cups peeled parsnips, sliced 1/4"
1 cup peeled Russett potato, sliced 1/4"
1 cup peeled beets, sliced thin
2 cups chicken or vegetable broth (gluten-free, if desired)
2 tbs. dark honey or brown sugar
2 tbs. cider vinegar
1/2 tsp. salt
1 tbs. minced fresh mint or 1 tsp. dried
sour cream for garnish

When CSAs give you roots, make something red! Heat oil in Dutch oven or skillet and sauté onions and cabbage over medium heat until soft, about 5 minutes. Combine root vegetables and broth and bring to boil. Add onions and cabbage and reduce to simmer, 20 minutes or until vegetables are soft. Stir in honey, vinegar, salt, and mint. Garnish individual servings with sour cream, if desired.

Main Dishes

Stuffed Squash
Lamb with Braised Fennel
and Delicata Sauce
A Very Sunny Curry
Gratifying Goulash

Stuffed Squash
Taste of Earth

Prep: 10 minutes Cook: 40 minutes Serves: 4

2 tbs. olive oil, divided
2 acorn squash
1 cup brown rice
1 cup vegetable stock
1 cup apple cider
1 cup finely chopped Asian mushrooms (wild option:
    hen of the woods mushrooms – cook thoroughly)
1 cup grated organic carrots
1/2 cup diced red onion
1/2 cup finely chopped kale
2 cloves garlic, chopped
1/2 tsp. salt

Preheat oven to 400°F. Cut squash in half, scoop out seeds
and strings, and brush with 1 tbs. olive oil. Place cut ends
down in baking dish and cook 35-40 minutes. Meanwhile,
combine rice, stock, and cider in sauce pan. Bring to boil,
then reduce heat to simmer, cooking 40 minutes, or until rice
is tender and liquid is absorbed. While that simmers, heat
remaining oil in large cast iron skillet or sauté pan. Sauté
mushrooms, onion, and carrots over med-low heat until onions are translucent, about ten minutes. Add kale and garlic
and cook five more minutes. Stir in salt, then mix thoroughly
with rice. Divide mixture between squash halves, garnishing
with parsley, if desired. Serve immediately, but squash may
be very hot.

Lamb with Braised Fennel and Delicata Sauce
Taste of Italy

Prep: 20 minutes Marinate: overnight Cook: 90 minutes Serves 2

1.5 lb. leg of lamb

Marinade:
1/2 cup Madeira or Sherry
1/4 cup grape seed oil
1/4 cup cider vinegar
1/2 cup chopped fennel stalks and leaves

Braised Fennel:
3 fennel bulbs, washed and quartered
1 tbs. butter
1 tbs. white sugar
1/2 tsp. salt
1/4 cup Madeira or Sherry

Sauce:
1/2 cup roasted Delicata squash (or acorn or butternut)
1/2 tsp. liquid smoke
1/4 cup goat cheese
2 tbs. light cream
1 tbs. minced fennel leaf

A special meal for two, or multiply recipe as needed. Mix marinade ingredients. Place lamb leg in zip-lock bag with marinade and seal, forcing out as much air as possible. Marinate in refrigerator overnight. Preheat oven to 450°F. Cut squash in half and remove seeds. Lightly spray with oil and place cut-side down on baking sheet. Remove lamb from bag and pat dry. Sprinkle with salt and pepper, if desired. Place lamb on rack over drip tray, fat side up. Cook lamb and squash at 450°F for 30 minutes. Remove squash to cool. Reduce heat to 300°F and cook lamb about one hour more. In last half hour of cooking, braise fennel bulbs: Melt butter in sauté pan over medium heat. Cook fennel bulbs until they start to brown, about five minutes per side. Sprinkle with sugar and salt, letting bulbs caramelize, one minute. Add Madeira and let cook down, about two minutes. For sauce, mix squash with liquid smoke, goat cheese, and cream in a small sauce pan over low heat, stirring constantly. Remove from heat and stir in fennel leaf. Let lamb sit 10 minutes before slicing. Spoon sauce over lamb slices. Serve with braised fennel bulbs and brown rice or roasted potatoes.

A Very Sunny Curry
Taste of India

Prep: 20 minutes Cook: 30 minutes Makes six servings

2 cups peeled, cubed buttercup squash
2 cups cooked brown rice
1/2 yellow onion, diced
1/2 cup golden raisins
1 tsp. curry
1/2 tsp. ginger
1/2 tsp. cinnamon
1/4-1/2 tsp. white pepper
1 tsp. salt
1 green apple, peeled and diced*
olive oil for cooking
yogurt for garnish (optional)

A different kind of stir-fry, this combines the spices of Asia with with sweetness of squash and bite of tart apple. Cook rice. Boil squash until tender, about 10 minutes, reserving liquid. Sauté onion in 1 tbs. olive oil until translucent, stirring frequently to prevent browning. Add squash, spices, raisins, and apple, stirring after each addition. Add cooked rice and mix well over med/low heat. If necessary, add reserved liquid to keep mixture from sticking to pan. Serve with broiled chicken or lamb or as a dish in itself. Top with plain yogurt, if desired.

* Wait to cut apple until last moment, or place pieces in cold water with a teaspoon of lemon juice to prevent browning.

Gratifying Goulash
Taste of Hungary Meets India

Prep: 20 minutes Cook: 1 hour Makes six servings

1.5 lb. stew beef, goat, mutton, or venison
1 tbs. olive oil
5 cups peeled, cubed butternut squash
1 yellow onion, sliced
1 tbs. tomato paste
1 cup dry red wine
2 tsp. garam masala (or 1/2 tsp each of black pepper,
  cardamom, cinnamon, coriander, cumin)
1 tsp. salt
1 1/2 tbs. smoked paprika

This stew has the traditional paprika spiked up with the Indian spice melange: garam masala. You can find this blend in most supermarkets and Indian specualty shops or make your own. Cardamom, the priciest ingredient on this list, also is great in baked goods and is used in many recipes in this book.

Preheat oven to 300°F. Sear meat in large skillet over medium heat with a tbs. of olive oil to prevent sticking, turning as needed. Remove meat to bowl. Add wine to skillet, stirring with meat juices. Add onions, tomato paste, and spices, cooking until just soft. Add squash and meat and stir well. Line a baking dish with foil, fill with mixture, then cover tightly with additional foil. Cook until squash is tender, about 50 minutes to an hour. Serve immediately, with rice or noodles, if desired.

Treats and Tips

Oatmeal Power Cookies
Jamaican Ginger Carrot Bread
Perfect Pumpkin Bread
Pumpkin Applesauce
Mercy Brown Bread
Harvesting Acorns for Fun and Protein
Storing Apples
Winter Baldwins

Oatmeal Power Cookies
Taste of Earth

1 stick butter, softened
1/2 cup brown sugar
1 cup whole wheat flour
2 cups oatmeal
1/2 tsp. salt
1 tsp. baking powder
1 tsp. each of cardamom, cinnamon, and/or nutmeg
1/2 cup milk
1/4 cup flax seeds (optional)
Add-Ins: 1/4-1/2 cup mini chocolate chips, walnuts, dried
  berries, orange peel, etc.

Preheat over to 375°F. Cream butter and sugar. Mix in dry ingredients except add-ins. Stir in milk. Blend in flax seed, nuts, etc. until well-incorporated. Drop by tablespoon onto baking sheet. Bake 8-10 minutes. Cool before storing.

Jamaican Ginger Carrot Bread
Taste of the Caribbean

Prep: 20 minutes Cook: 25 to 60 minutes Makes: 4 small loaves,
    25 muffins, or one bundt cake

2 eggs or 1/2 cup of apple sauce
1/2 cup vegetable oil
1/2 cup brown sugar
1/4 cup molasses
2 cups peeled, grated, organic carrots (4-6)
2 cups peeled, grated, fresh or stored apples
1 tbs. minced ginger (include juice)*
2 cups unbleached flour
1 cup whole wheat flour
1 tsp. fresh ground nutmeg**
2 tsp. baking powder
1/2 tsp. salt
1/2 cup of milk or water
1/2 cup raisins (optional)
1/2 cup chopped walnuts (optional)
1/4 cup flax seed (optional)

This is a Jamaican-inspired bread that also includes apples and carrots for a very moist, almost cake-like texture. Preheat oven to 375°F. Beat eggs (or apple sauce)
and oil with an electric mixer until the consistency of
pudding. Mix in sugars, then ginger, carrots, and apples.
Sift flours, nutmeg, baking powder, and salt in a separate
bowl, then add dry mix in small amount to wet mix,

blending with mixer after each addition. Stir in milk or water, and raisins, flax seeds, or nuts, if using. Grease pans or tins and fill half-way (use all of batter for bundt cake). Cook 40-45 minutes for four small loaves, 20-25 minutes for muffins, 1 hour for bundt cake, or until toothpick comes out clean.

* Use a spoon to peel ginger.

Perfect Pumpkin Bread
Taste of Earth

3 cups flour
2 tsp. baking soda
1 1/2 tsp. salt
1 tsp. fresh ground nutmeg
1 tsp. cardamom
2 1/2 cups sugar
1 cup cooking oil or apple sauce for lower-fat version
4 eggs or 5 egg whites for lower-fat version
1 15 oz. can of pumpkin
2/3 cups water

Optional:
1 cup chopped walnuts
1 cup chocolate chips

Sift all dry ingredients except sugar in medium-sized bowl. In larger bowl, beat eggs, sugar, oil, and water until smooth. Add pumpkin and beat, then add flour mixture in small mounts, beating after each addition. Fold in nuts and/or chocolate chips. Divide batter between three greased and floured coffee cans* and bake 1 hour 30 minutes at 300°F. Cool cans ten minutes in wire racks or towels, then remove bread. Wrap in foil and keep refrigerated until ready to use. Slice when completely cool. Serve with a Thanksgiving feast or spread with cream cheese for a hearty breakfast.

* Use coffee cans without overlapping rims or use 3 large bread pans.

Pumpkin Applesauce
Taste of New England

1 3-4 lb baking pumpkin (Baby Pam, Cinderella, Long Island
 Cheese, Nantucket/Long Pie, NE Pie) (yields about 3.5 cups)
5 apples (try a mix of Braeburn, Cortland, Crispin (Mutsu), Fuji,
 Gala, Golden Delicious, Jazz, Jonagold, Liberty, McIntosh,
 Melrose
1 tsp. cinnamon
1 tsp. ginger
1/2 cup brown sugar
1 tbs. lemon juice
olive oil

Preheat oven to 425°F. Wash pumpkin, cut off stem, and cut in half. Scoop out seeds. (Save for roasted seeds on page 175.) Pierce outer skin with fork several times. Brush insides with olive oil. Place cut-side down on baking sheet and cook 40-60 minutes, depending on size of pumpkin. When pumpkin is soft (yields to pressure from fork), remove from oven to cool. Peel, core, and dice apples. Heat large sauce pan over medium heat with a tbs. of olive oil. Add apples, spices, sugar, and about a half cup of water, mixing well. When apples get soft enough (15-20 minutes), scoop out cooled pumpkin and mix in thoroughly with apples, using an immersion blender. Stir in lemon juice. Makes app. 7 cups.

Great by itself, or added to muffins, oatmeal, or toast.

Mercy Brown Bread
Taste of Old New England

Prep: 10 minutes Cook: 2 hours Makes 3 loaves

1 cup processed acorns (see page 134) or raw hazelnuts
1 cup buttermilk
1 cup plain yogurt
1/2 cup molasses
1 cup fresh cranberries
1 cup unbleached flour
1 cup whole wheat flour
2 tsp. baking powder
1/2 tsp. salt
1 tsp. cinnamon

Combine nuts and buttermilk and run through food processor to make a thick paste. Mix paste with yogurt and molasses. Stir in washed and picked over cranberries, removing stems and soft berries first. In a separate bowl, whisk together flours, baking soda, salt, and cinnamon. Gradually stir flour mixture into wet mixture. Grease three coffee cans and divide batter between them. Seal cans with foil and rubber bands.

Place cans in large stock pot with at least two inches of water. Cover and bring to gentle boil. Steam breads two hours, adding more water as necessary. Allow to cool before removing foil. Slice and serve.

About Mercy Brown

Mary Brown had the misfortune of dying of consumption (tuberculosis) in 1888, shortly following her mother. Two years later, her brother Edwin became sick with the same feared illness. Mercy Brown was next, dying in 1892, so naturally the family suspected vampirism. One of the last documented cases in New England, the father George Brown was persuaded to exhume his daughter Mercy for evidence of vampirism. (Some accounts say the older sister and mother were exhumed as well, but a family descendent states this was not the case.) Being the most recently dead and in frozen ground or possibly a crypt, she looked unchanged. One account implies the body had moved in the coffin, and as embalming was not common, gas and fluids in the body could have caused this. Finding liquid blood in the heart only confirmed their suspicions of vampirism. Her heart was removed, burnt on a nearby rock, and mixed with water to be administered to Edwin to cure him. He died two months later. The story inspired several tales, books and movies, including H.P. Lovecraft's "The Shunned House" and Bram Stroker's "Dracula" (where Lucy is supposedly based on her). Mercy Brown is buried in Chestnut Hill Cemetery in Exeter, RI. If you still have an appetite after this, try this recipe that reflects the times. The acorns represent what gets stored in the cold and buried. The cranberries, being red, you can probably guess.

Harvesting Acorns for Fun & Protein
(or, "Why Should the Squirrels Have All the Fun?")

By Ryk McIntyre

If you live anywhere near oak trees, and there's a good chance of that in the Northern Hemisphere, then you live close to a great source of protein. In the Northeast there are three common types of oaks: the Red, the White & the Black Oak. The oaks vary in bitterness (due to tannin levels) with Black Oaks being the most bitter and White so sweet, they can be sometimes eaten right out of the shell.

After harvesting, shell and look over each nut. If there is a hole in the side, or it looks blackened inside, discard. It means acorn weevil eggs were laid there, and the meat of the nut was eaten by the larva. Next, you will need to leech out the tannins. This can be done by putting them in a mesh-bag and letting them sit in fresh, flowing water for a few days, or by boiling the acorns. To boil acorns, place in a large pot with plenty of water. As water darkens (the tannins), change it out with fresh water until water remains clear. This may take 2-4 hours, depending on the tannin levels in your acorns, and how many pounds you are processing at once. You'll know they're done when you can eat one without it tasting bitter. Finally, roast nuts slowly at 175°F for about 2 hours, checking often. You want them to be dry roasted, but not burnt.

Once processed, they can be used in pancakes, brown bread, or ground in a food processor to make a flour/meal. Refrigerated, they last quite a while, but for best results, use them within a week or so.

Also, bar your windows from squirrels. They take this personally.

STORING APPLES

Apples were brought to America by European settlers. They thrive in cool climates, thus their prevalence in New England. My personal favorites are Cortland and Ginger Crisp. We pick apples every year, celebrating with a pie or two, eating apples daily, making apple sauce, and storing some for the winter.

Apples can be available year round with careful storage. Home-stored apples should keep until February. Choose only unblemished or bruised, under-ripe and tart apples, such as Baldwin, Crispin, Ida Red, Jonathans, Northern Spy, Red Delicious, Rome, Stayman, Turley, Winter Banana, and Winesap. Wash and completely dry apples. Wrap tightly in newspaper or perforated plastic bag and store in a root cellar away from potatoes and onions, around 30-32°F and with 90% humidity. Be careful not to let the apples freeze or their cell walls will burst. Many Rhode Island orchards now store apples in a temperature- and humidity-controlled facility and make them available at farmer's markets.

Winter Baldwins

by Joyce Heon

Their value was in winter keeping.
They held the woody fibers
of spring long into the fall,
cherishing their bronzy green
until the summer sun began
its slide into winter.
Many barely blushed at all,
held hard to the limbs,
needed yanking to harvest.
Like the boscs, they wanted
a brush with the frost before picking.

You sit in a silence that
discomfits neither you nor I,
these quiet days where
anticipation wanes. There is
a comfort to their sameness,
where demands are the simple
needs that hold together to
the next day's wakening.
You have known the upstream
of life long enough, become
a long-distance swimmer,
pacing your greased body
to the rest of a safe port.

Hard they came to crates.
Hard they sat in the winter
chill of the earthen cellar.
Some pied Thanksgiving,
more at Christmas.
Come January, they had shrunk,
reduced their flavors into

a spice of juiceless pulp
in wizened skin it took
carnivore teeth to pierce.

It is her hair, dense and lustrous,
that calls your hand out of repose,
but the abundant power of youth
brushes away the sight of you
in dutiful sheet changing.
Accented chatter,
orchestrated cheerful,
is less kindness than strain
on your diminished hearing.
I want to ask her to bend her
head to your hand, let you stroke
the mane of youth that falls
over her shoulder, but this is
more kindness than she has
understanding to give.

In January we rummaged
the crate for the few
red baldwins, savored
their un-apple-like flavor.
Mother, do you recall
the last of the box,
woody fibers, steeped
in the juices of living,
life holding beyond its season?
Can you taste the memory
of baldwins in winter?

Rather than a barren season, there is much available with careful planning. All the goods prepared and canned from the summer and autumn await to be opened and enjoyed. Vegetables blanched and frozen from the summer awake from hibernation. Apples picked in autumn await as canned apple sauce, or wrapped individually in newspaper in a root cellar. Many farms use climate-controlled storage for fall crops. Winter squash will keep for months in a cool basement. Dried legumes can be soaked into soup. Nuts add protein. Meats are thawed. Many of these winter recipes could be made any time. What's in Season: Apples (stored) • Arugula • Beets • Bok Choy • Broccoli • Brussels Sprouts • Cabbage • Carrots • Cauliflower • Celeriac • Chard • Cider • Collards • Dried Fruit • Frozen Fruit • Frozen Vegetables • Garlic • Granola • Honey • Kale • Leeks • Maple Syrup • Microgreens • Mushrooms (fresh and dried): Crimini, Oyster, Portabella • Nuts • Onions • Parsnips • Potatoes • Potted Herbs • Salad Greens • Shallots • Sprouts • Sweet Potatoes • Turnips • Winter Squash • Dairy:

WINTER

Cheese (cow, goat) • Eggs (chicken, duck, goose) • Milk (cow, goat) • Yogurt (cow, goat) • Meat: Beef • Chicken • Duck • Fowl • Goat • Lamb • Pork • Turkey • Seafood: Butterfish • Cod • Crab • Flounder • Haddock • Littleneck Clams • Lobster • Mackerel • Monkfish • Mussels • Oysters • Pollock • Quahogs • Scallops • Sea Bass • Sea Robins • Seaweed • Shrimp • Skate Wings • Squid • Steamers • Striped Bass • Swordfish • Tuna What's to Do: Hang Bells on Trees to Welcome the Sun's Return at Winter Solstice and Ring in the New Year • Build a Snow Witch: Top with a Pointy Hat and Watch It Melt! • Ice Skating • Ice Fish for Stocked Trout and Salmon • Visit the Winter Market • Make an Oven-Full of Roasted Root Vegetables • Play "Block of Ice!": Freeze Water In a Container, Remove, and Kick Around the Deck or Driveway • Make Candles • Make Recycled Crayons By Melting Crayon Pieces In a Silicone Mold on a Cookie Sheet at 250°F 20-40 Minutes or Until Completely Melted. Cool On Counter or Outside. • Make a Pine Cone Bird Feeder • Watch and Identify Winter Birds • Find and Identify Animal Tracks in the Snow • Make Gingerbread Cookies and Donate Them • Buy Local Art and Hand-Made Goods

Salads, Sides, and Soups

Baby Got Bok Choy
Carnival Gold Frittata
Hummus
Rainbow Roasted Fries
Croquettes
Barley Cakes
Boxty Latkes
Money Bags
Red Lentil Soup
Curried Cashew Squash Soup
Seafood Spinach Stew

Gluten-Free/Low Sodium/Vegetarian Option

Baby Got Bok Choy
Taste of Thai

Prep: 15 minutes Cook: 30 minutes Serves 4

1 cup gluten-free vegetable or chicken broth
2 tbs. Mirin or white wine (such as Newport Great White)
2 tsp. corn starch
1 tbs. sesame oil
1 lb. shelled, de-veined local shrimp, squid, or firm tofu
1 small yellow onion, diced
1/2 cup chopped white mushrooms
8-10 washed baby bok choy, chopped into 1/2" pieces
1/2 cup chopped fresh cilantro
2" peeled, minced ginger (use a spoon)
2 tbs. lime juice (about one lime), plus lime for garnish
Spice it up: 1 tsp red pepper flakes or Sriracha sauce (found
    in Asian markets) (optional)

Whisk broth, Mirin or wine, and corn starch. Set aside. In a large sauté pan with lid, heat sesame oil on medium-high and stir-fry shrimp until cooked through, 3-5 minutes. Set aside. Sauté onions and mushrooms 2-3 minutes. Add bok choy and pour broth over all.

Cover and cook 6-8 minutes, stirring up from the bottom occasionally. Reduce to simmer. Add shrimp, squid, or tofu, cilantro, ginger, and lime, stirring well. Heat gently 10 minutes, stirring occasionally to prevent sticking. Serve with jasmine rice and lime wedges.

Carnival Gold Frittata
Taste of Italy

Prep: 10 minutes Total Cook Time: 50-80 minutes Serves 6

1 carnival or winter squash
1 medium yellow onion, diced
6 large eggs
1 cup grated Narragansett Creamery Atwell's Gold
1 tbs. dried lemon thyme
1/2 tsp. salt
1/2 tsp. cayenne
oil for cooking

Preheat oven to 375°F. Cut squash in half and scoop out seeds. Save seeds for planting, compost, or make roasted seeds (page 175). Brush cut sides with olive oil and cook face down in baking dish, 30-60 minutes, depending on size of squash. Squash are cooked when fork pierces skin easily. Set aside to cool. Heat one tbs. oil in oven-safe pan or cast-iron skillet. Sauté onions until translucent. Loosely beat eggs in large bowl and stir in cheese, thyme, salt, and cayenne. Pour into pan with onions.   Add squash by shredding from skin with a fork. Cook over med-low heat until almost set, 10-15 minutes. Place pan in oven and broil 1-3 minutes to brown.

Hummus
Taste of the Middle East

Prep: 10 minutes Serves 8-10

15 oz. can of chick peas
5 tbs. lemon juice
3 tbs. tahini
2 tbs. olive oil
1 tsp. cumin
1/4 tsp. salt

While I can't claim local ingredients for this recipe, making it yourself will result in less plastic in the landfill. The can the chick peas come in is recyclable. Lemon juice and olive oil are common staples in most American households. You can find tahini in most markets today, usually with organic or ethnic foods, but the recipe can be made without it. You can also mix in diced red pepper, garlic, basil, or parsley. Hummus is a good source of protein, iron, dietary fiber, and vitamin C.

Drain and rinse chick peas. Place all ingredients in blender or food processor. Blend until smooth. Great with cucumbers, celery, carrots, peppers, tomatoes, pita chips, and more! I sometimes make "spider sandwiches" with cucumber slices and carrot stick legs for the kids.

Rainbow Roasted Fries
Taste of the Earth

Prep: 10 minutes Total Cook Time: 25-40 minutes Serves 6

3-4 red potatoes
1 sweet potato
2 Yukon Gold potatoes
5-6 blue potatoes
olive oil
salt, pepper, paprika

Preheat oven to 425°F. Cut vegetables into french fries., leaving skins on. Place fries in a large food storage container. Drizzle with olive oil and season with salt, pepper, and paprika to taste. Seal with lid and shake vigorously to coat. Spread fries in a single layer on a cookie sheet. Cook until crisp, 25-40 minutes, turning fries with spatula once during cooking. In the summer, this recipe works well with zucchini.

Croquettes
Taste of France Meets Italy

Prep: 10 minutes Cook: 30-35 minutes Chill overnight Makes 12

1/2 diced onion
1 tbs. unsalted butter
1 cup uncooked risotto
3 cups no-salt chicken stock
1/2 tsp. salt
1/4 tsp. white pepper

1/2 cup grated Naragansett
Atwell's
 Gold or aged parmesan
2 eggs, beaten and divided
1 cup Panko crumbs
1 tsp. lemon thyme
oil for frying

Melt butter. Sauté onions over medium heat until golden, 3-5 minutes. Stir in risotto and cook 1 minute, stirring frequently. Pour in one cup of stock, cooking and stirring until absorbed. Continue with second cup of stock. Repeat with last cup of stock. Add liquid and cook longer if rice is not tender after that. Stir in cheese, salt, and pepper. Chill several hours or overnight. This will form better patties. When cool, mix rice with one beaten egg. Form mixture into 2 1/2 inch patties, using wet hands. Mix crumbs with lemon thyme in a shallow dish. Set second beaten egg in a separate shallow dish. Dip patties in egg, then crumbs, keeping spaced apart on a tray. Heat 1/4" of oil in a large skillet on high. Place patties gently in oil (the level will rise as more are added), and cook in two batches, about a minute per side, or until golden. Lift out with a slotted spatula to a wire rack over a tray. Serve hot.

Barley Cakes
Taste of Ireland

Prep: 40 minutes Cook: 20 minutes Makes 24 meatless cakes, 36
  meat cakes.

3/4 cup cooked barley
1/2 cup unbleached flour
1 cup natural oatmeal
1 medium onion, diced and sautéed
1 tsp. fresh ground coriander
1/2 tsp. each salt and white pepper
1 tsp. dried thyme
1 cup milk or vegan substitute
1 lb. ground pork or one cup of textured vegetable
  protein (optional)

This is a take on the classic white puddings or Ireland,
which are sausages boiled, sliced, and fried. Cook barley according to package directions. This can be done a
day ahead. Preheat oven to 350°F. Mix ingredients thoroughly. Bake in greased mini-muffin tins 20 minutes.

Boxty Latkes
Taste of Ireland Meets Jewish Russia

Prep: 25 minutes Cook: 30 minutes Makes 28 four inch pancakes

2 pounds organic Yukon
  Gold potatoes
1 medium organic onion, diced
1 organic carrot, grated
1 tsp. fresh ground coriander
1/2 tsp. each salt and white pepper

1 cup buttermilk (or vegan
  substitute)
1 cup unbleached flour
lemon juice
1 tbs. butter or olive oil
oil for cooking

Did you know potatoes are full of vitamins, particularly the skins? Cut up 3-4 scrubbed potatoes, leaving skins on. Boil until tender, 10-15 minutes. Meanwhile, saute onions and carrots in butter or olive oil until golden and set aside. Grate 2-3 scrubbed potatoes into bowl with cold water and a splash of lemon juice to prevent discoloration, also leaving skins on. Drain in colander, pressing down with masher and squeezing water out with hands just before adding to batter. Mash drained boiled potatoes with buttermilk, vegetables, and seasonings. Stir in grated potato. Add flour a little at a time, until absorbed. Batter should be thick. Heat 1/4" of oil in large skillet over medium heat. Drop batter by spoonful, cooking 4 inch pancakes 2-3 minutes per side. Drain on towels. (Pancakes can be kept warm on a cookie tray in a 250°F oven.) Serve with butter, breakfast meats, sour cream, and/or apple sauce.

Money Bags
Taste of China Meets Greece

Prep: 20 minutes Cook: 20 minutes Makes 48

Filling:
1/4 cup dried Asian mushrooms, reconstituted in boiling
  water 10 minutes (reserve liquid)
6 oz. frozen spinach
1/4 cup pine nuts or sunflower seeds
1-2 tbs. oil
4 tsp. butter
1 tsp. dried thyme
1/8 tsp. pepper
2 scallions, or onion, chopped fine
4 oz. local feta (such as Narragansett Creamery's Salty Sea)

Celebrate the New Year, Chinese or otherwise, with this appetizer of prosperity. The spinach in these dumplings represents cash, with feta, pine nuts or seeds, and thyme adding a punch of flavor inside. You can by-pass using a bamboo steamer by placing a cookie rack on the bottom of a large stock pot with lid. Use wax paper pierced with holes and brushed with oil to keep wraps from sticking. You can even tie bags with a thread of green scallion for a nice little detail.

Chop mushrooms very fine. Sauté pine nuts or seeds in 1 tbs. oil, until lightly toasted. Add spinach and mush-room liquid as needed, cooking down, about 10 minutes.

Stir in mushrooms, butter, thyme, and pepper. When all is incorporated, stir in scallions and feta. Remove from heat and let cool.

Dough:
2 cups flour (or Gluten-Free All-Purpose Flour)
1 tsp. baking powder
1 tsp. salt
1 egg
1/2 cup water
1 tbs. oil

Sift dry ingredients. Beat egg, water, and oil in bowl. Add to dry ingredients and knead into a stiff dough. Cover bowl with a damp towel and let rest 10 minutes to activate baking powder. Form dough into two foot snake and cut into 48 slices. Roll each slice into a thin round, add a tablespoon of filling, gather dough edges, and twist to seal. (Use a drop of water if money bags do not stay closed.) Place dumplings in oiled bamboo basket or oiled, pierced wax paper on a cooling rack over simmering but not boiling water, 12-15 minutes. Serve immediately.

Red Lentil Soup
Taste of Egypt

Prep: 15 minutes Cook: 40 minutes Makes about 4 quarts

2 tbs. olive oil
1/2 medium onion, diced
1 large carrot, peeled and sliced into 1" half-moons
3 celery stalks, sliced thin, or 2/3 cup grated celeriac
1 tsp. ground cumin
1 tsp. coriander
1 tsp. cinnamon
1/2 tsp. ancho chili powder
52 oz. Pomi chopped tomatoes (cans may leach BPAs)
3 cups red lentils, picked over (about 1 pound)

Heat oil in large pot over medium heat. Add onion, carrot, and celery, stirring and cooking until softened, about 5 minutes. Stir in spices and cook until fragrant, 2-3 minutes. Pour in tomatoes and heat another 2-3 minutes. Add lentils and 8 cups of water and bring to a gentle boil. Reduce heat and simmer, uncovered, until lentils are soft and soup is thick. Puree in batches in a blender or use an immersion blender. Serve as a soup with yogurt garnish and warm pita, injera, or sourdough bread. Also a great side dish with eggs or as a sauce over oven-roasted potatoes.

Curried Cashew Squash Soup
Taste of America Meets India

Prep: 15 minutes Cook: 35-40 minutes Serves 4

2 tbs. olive oil, divided
1/2 onion, diced
1 cup sliced celery (about 5 stalks)
1 tsp. yellow curry
1 cup raw unsalted cashews
4 cups of peeled orange winter squash, cut into 1" cubes
optional: 1 tbs. tahini

Heat 1 tbs. of oil in large pot. Add onions and celery, stirring frequently over medium-low heat until onions begin to caramelized, 8-10 minutes. (Sprinkle in sugar to speed up the process.) Mix in curry power and heat until fragrant. Add squash and 3 cups of water. Bring to a simmer and cook until squash is soft, 20-25 minutes. Meanwhile, heat remaining oil in skillet over medium-low heat. Toss in cashews and lightly toast. Transfer cashews to food processor and grind to a paste. When squash is cooked, puree mixture with immersion blender, then stir in cashews. Add tahini if desired.

Seafood Spinach Stew
Taste of Italy

Prep: 10 minutes Cook: 30 minutes Serves 6

1 tbs. olive oil
1 yellow onion, diced
1 clove garlic, minced
1 small celeriac, cut into 1" cubes
10 oz. frozen spinach, thawed and drained or 2 cups fresh
1/2 tsp. dried marjoram
salt and pepper to taste
1 cup chicken broth
1 lb. flounder or mild fish, cut into 1" pieces
1 lb. blue mussels or clams
1/2 lb. bay scallops

Sauté celeriac, onions and garlic in 1 tbs. olive oil in a large skillet or Dutch oven over medium heat until translucent. Add spinach, marjoram, salt, and pepper, cooking down. Add broth and fish, cooking until almost opaque. Add rinsed mussels and scallops. Cook until mussels open and all seafood looks opaque, about five minutes. Serve with rice, if desired.

Main Dishes

Great White Skate
French Meat Pie
Smoked Paprika Stroganoff
Poulet de Terre

Great White Skate
Taste of France

Prep: 5 minutes Cook: 10 minutes Serves 4

1 skate wing, cut into four equal pieces
1/2 cup unbleached flour
3 tbs. butter
1/3 cup Newport Great White wine
fresh chopped parsley

The local wine gives this classic brown butter dish its uniqueness without competing with the delicate scallop flavor of skate, often caught as fishermen pursue other fish. It's simple, quick, and more affordable than some other seafood. Cut prepared wing into four steaks. Dredge in flour, shaking off excess. Heat a large sauté pan over medium heat. Add butter and melt, turning pan around, until lightly brown. Place skate gently in butter, cooking until opaque three-quarter's through, about five minutes. Flip carefully and cook 3-5 minutes more. Add wine and cook off, scraping up crispy bits from the pan, about two minutes. Be careful to not overcook. Add chopped parsley and transfer to plates gently. Great with risotto.

French Meat Pie

Taste of French-Canada

Pie Crust (see page 8)

Filling:
3/4 lbs. lean ground beef
3/4 lbs. lean ground pork
1/8 tsp. each of ground dried marjoram and/or oregano,
    rosemary, sage, and thyme
1/2 medium onion, diced
1/2 cup unseasoned bread-crumbs
1/2 tsp. each of salt and pepper
1 tbs. oil

This is a variation of a recipe handed down from my grandmother. (See page 171 on how to dry herbs.) Bell's Seasoning could also be substituted, which is what she used. Heat oil on medium-high in a large sauté pan. Sauté onions until translucent. Add meat and brown. Stir in salt, pepper, and seasoning, first draining excess fat from meat if necessary. Add bread-crumbs to absorb remaining moisture. Put in prepared pastry shell. Top with pastry crust, cutting a five-point "star" of slits around top. Bake at 350°F for 35-40 minutes.

Smoked Paprika Stroganov
Taste of 19th Century Russia

Prep: 10 minutes Cook: 30-40 minutes Makes six servings

1 cup sliced mushrooms
1/2 diced yellow onion
1 tbs. butter
1 tbs. olive oil
1 tbs. or more of smoked paprika
1 tsp. salt
1 cup chicken or beef broth
1/2 cup red wine
2 tbs. flour
1/2 cup sour cream
1 lb. ground beef, pork, or lamb

Melt butter in Dutch oven or large sauté pan over medium heat. Add mushroom and cook gently, stirring to coat with butter, about five minutes. Add onions, stirring, and cook until they begin to caramelize, 10-15 minutes. Stir flour into mushroom mix until well-combined, then add broth. Meanwhile, heat oil in separate skillet and brown meat in small batches, sprinkling with paprika and salt. Set meat aside. After meat is cooked, deglaze pan with wine. Add drippings to mushroom mix, then stir in meat and sour cream, adding more paprika if desired. Serve with peas and egg noodles, other pasta, or oven fries.

Poulet de Terre

Taste of France and New Orleans

Prep: 10 minutes Cook: 50-60 minutes Makes 6-8 servings

Sauce:
4 tbs. butter or olive oil
1 yellow onion, diced
5 stalks of washed, chopped celery, or 1 cup grated celeriac
1 cup peeled, chopped carrots
2 cloves of garlic, minced
2 tbs. brown sugar
1/2 cup Madeira wine
3-4 cups gluten-free chicken or vegetable broth
4 oz. goat cheese
1 tsp. ancho chili powder

Sliced tempeh or six to eight chicken breasts, fat trimmed*
1 cup flour (or gluten-free substitute)
2 tbs. paprika
1/2 tsp. cumin
1/2 tsp. garlic powder
1/8 tsp. cayenne
1/4 tsp. salt

Melt butter (or heat oil) in stock pot over medium heat. Add onion, celery/celeriac, and carrots and cook until vegetables wilt. When onions start to crisp, mix in brown sugar and garlic. Cook five minutes, stirring occasionally. Deglaze pan with Madeira wine. Add broth and cook, uncovered, until liquid is reduced by half, 30-40 minutes. For thinner sauce, add more broth.

Meanwhile, blend spices for chicken/tempeh and mix with flour.   Tenderize chicken by piercing all over with knife or blade tenderizer.   Dredge protein and cook in sauté pan over medium heat in 1-2 tbs. olive oil, turning when meat is cooked 3/4 through.

Using an immersion blender or carefully transferring sauce to blender in small amounts, purée vegetables. Return to pan and reduce heat to low. Add ancho chili powder and goat cheese, stirring until cheese is dissolved. Serve sauce over chicken or tempeh, with choice of starch.

*This recipe also works well with rolled and baked sole or sautéed shrimp.

Treats

Rosemary Rounds
Curried Popcorn
Yule Dates

Rosemary Rounds
Taste of Earth

Prep: 5 minutes Cook: 20 minutes Makes 48 cookies

1/2 cup softened, unsalted butter
1/2 cup dark brown sugar
1/2 cup finely chopped walnuts
1 tsp. minced fresh rosemary
1 tsp. vanilla extract
1 tsp. lemon juice
1 1/2 cups unbleached flour

Pre-heat oven to 300°F. Cream together butter and sugar. Mix in remaining ingredients in order listed. Press dough into greased mini-muffin tins, filling half-way. Cook 18-20 minutes, or until just golden. Cool and carefully remove from tins. Store in air-tight container.

Curried Popcorn
Taste of India Meets Indians

Prep: 1 minute Cook: 8-10 minutes Makes about 12 cups

2 tbs. olive oil
2 tbs. butter
1 tsp. organic sweet yellow curry
1 tsp. sugar
dash of salt (or to taste)
1/2 cup non-GMO popcorn kernels

Avoid PFOAs from microwave popcorn and save money while making your own! (Plus, it will taste better.) Melt olive oil and butter over medium heat in large sauce pan. Stir in curry, sugar, and salt. Add popcorn and cover. Shake mix back and forth off of burner to mix. Return to heat and wait for popping to start, in about 3-4 minutes. Lift pan and shake as before. Return to heat. Popping will continue in a Bell curve: a little at first, then build to very rapid, finally subsiding to nothing. Shake pan more frequently during rapid popping to keep kernels coated in flavorings and prevent burning. When you hear less than three pops per second, get ready to pour into large bowl. You can pour off what's already popped to cook the last few kernels. This recipe is highly addictive!

Yule Dates
Taste of Pakistan

Prep: 15 minutes Makes about 50

10 oz. pitted dates, room temperature
4 oz. local creamy goat cheese
1/4 cup finely chopped walnuts
2 tbs. finely chopped dried cranberries
1 tsp. finely chopped fresh rosemary

Mix all ingredients except dates thoroughly. Hold date firmly and make a shallow cut down length of narrow side. Gently pry open and fill with cheese mixture, using one side of a butter knife. Repeat with remaining dates. Garnish plate with a sprig of rosemary and fresh or dried cranberries.

TIPS & TRICKS

How to Dry Herbs:

Collection: Cut no more than a third off tips of plant before it flowers if using leaves. This is best done on a dry morning free of dew and before the sun evaporates volatile oils of herb. Many leaf herbs are ready to harvest in late May into mid-June. For flowers such as lavender or chamomile, harvest shortly after flowers open for best potency, also on a dry morning, usually in mid- to late summer. For seeds such as dill and coriander, let seeds fully mature and dry on the live plant, cut entire stalk, then rub off seeds into a paper bag.

Drying: Tightly bind leaf and flower herbs at base (herbs will shrink as they dry) with a twist-tie and hang upside-down to dry in a dark, cool place. I use a clothe line with binder clips in my basement, which thankfully is not damp. Drying will take between one and two weeks. Larger leaves such as sage and mullein may take longer. For loose or tiny pieces, you can dry in a mesh produce or laundry bag.

Storage: Herbs are ready to store in a jar, plastic bag, or envelope when completely dry. Leaves may be removed from stems using clean, dry hands and pulling leaves downward from stem. Rubbing stems between hands will remove small leaves quickly, but will still leave some on stem. I like to prep dry leaves over a towel so they don't blow away. Leaves can be kept whole or crushed. Keep away from heat and light. Herbs should keep for one year. Label and date.

How to Use Herbs:

Herbs Best Used Fresh: Basil, Cilantro, Parsley, Tarragon

Herbs Best Used Dry: Marjoram, Oregano, Thyme

Measurement: Use twice as much fresh herbs as it calls for dried in a recipe. Conversely, use half as much dried as it calls for fresh. Drying herbs concentrates the flavor.

Storage: Store dried herbs up to one year in air-tight, dry container away from light or heat. Store fresh herbs in ice cubes or keep in glass of water in refrigerator. Store pesto without cheese in freezer bag in freezer. Thaw bag in warm water.

Overnight Cheese:

Take a colander and line it with damp clean cheese cloth. Place colander over a bowl to collect whey. Empty a 32 oz. container of plain organic yogurt (or less) into lined colander. Weigh down yogurt with a freezer bag filled with water. Let stand overnight to drain. Use whey to replace any water used in breads, pizza dough, or to water plants. Remaining soft cheese in colander can be mixed with fresh chopped herbs and a pinch of salt or with berry jam and used as a stuffing in crêpes.

Cooking with Cast Iron:

Cast iron pans need to be seasoned before first using, but they retain heat well and will even add iron to foods cooked in them. To season, rub interior of pan with vegetable shortening or lard, then heat pan in oven at 350°F for one hour. Wipe cooled pan with paper towels or a clean rag designated for this purpose. After pan has been seasoned, preheat pan on stove, using a little oil. Since cast iron retains heat well, you may be able to turn heat off and still cook with it. This works well for quick-cook foods such as eggs. If you are done cooking, transfer pan to a cool surface on the stove or a trivet to avoid overcooking. Pan itself will be hot. Use an oven mitt to move pan or transfer it into or out of the oven. Wash pan with hot water and a soapy sponge, but do not leave wet, as water will remove the seasoning and cause pan to rust. For burnt on food, salt can be used to scour pan. Do not use scouring pads, because they will remove finish. Dry well before storing.

Cooking School:

Roasting Root Vegetables:
Wash and peel vegetables (except potatoes) and cut into 1/2"-1" pieces. Spray or toss with olive oil, salt, pepper, paprika, or other seasonings. Cook in oven-safe dish or cookie sheet at 450°F 40 to 70 minutes, turning once during roasting. Vegetables are done when fork-soft.

Roasting Winter Squash:
Wash squash and cut in half. Scoop out seeds and pulp. Poke holes with fork all over skin and brush olive oil on cut side. Place cut-side down in oven-safe dish or cookie sheet at 425°F 40 to 70 minutes, depending on size of squash.

Sautéing Greens:
Heat a tbs. of oil or fat in pan. Sauté onions and garlic first, if using. Add washed, chopped greens, stirring and cooking down until tender-crisp. Use water or broth to prevent sticking. Chicken broth tempers bitterness of some greens. Great for Romaine, dandelion and radish greens, and kale.

Roasting Seeds:
Mix any type of squash seeds with melted butter and Worcestershire sauce. Over low heat, cook seeds until glazed, stirring frequently.

Wild Foods:

Disclaimer: This list is a compilation of research and experience. It is vital you correctly identify your food and prepare it correctly! Two plants may have identical looking leaves, but grow staggered rather than paired. Two mushrooms may have similar-looking caps but different stems, one being edible and the other deadly. I have not included pictures because of this; consult an experienced wild food gatherer who can physically show you foods, explain how and where they grow, what they smell and taste like, which parts are edible, and how much is safe. For instance, juniper berries are edible, and used to make gin, but too many are toxic and will stress the kidneys of people with certain health problems. Some foods also cause allergies. Also, use common sense when you gather. If a plant is growing by a highway, it will most likely have pesticides, road salt, and carcinogens. Gathering plants here is also illegal, for the simple fact you may get hit by a car. Other roadsides and polluted areas should also be avoided. Sometimes the best thing you can do is gather the seeds and grow it at home in soil you've had tested for contaminants. A good reference is <u>Stalking the Wild Asparagus</u> by Ewel McGregor.

LEAVES

Chickweed, Comfrey, Dandelion, Lamb's Quarters, Mustard, Pine Needles (tea), Purslane, Sage, Thyme

FLOWERS

Borage, Cattail, Chicory, Dandelion (for wine), Rose (including hips), Violet, Calendula, Nasturtium

ROOTS

Chicory, Wild Carrot, Wild Parsnip, Greater Burdock

BERRIES/FRUIT

Apples (crab), Blackberries, Blueberries (wild berries are tiny but more flavorful), Grapes (Concord and Fox), Juniper Berries, Raspberries, Strawberries

SAP

Sugar Maple, Pine

SEEDS/NUTS

Acorn, Chestnut, Hazelnut, Nasturtium (pickle for caper substitute), Pine-nut, Sunflower

Companion Planting to Attract Beneficial Insects and Repel Pests

Most herbs attract pollinating insects with their flowers. Some of the stronger-smelling ones repel pests to various degrees. Slugs do not like the smell of anything from the allium family: chives, garlic, and onions. Many beetles and flies steer clear of mints and plants containing pyrethrum. By planting these with plants prone to pests, you may offer some protection. Be sure that the plants all require the same light, water, and soil conditions. An unhealthy plant will not thrive even when surrounded by the best of friends!

GREAT ATTRACTORS:

ASTER: Attracts pollinators.
BEE BALM: Attracts pollinators. Great for tomatoes. Keep away from peas and squash (may spread powdery mildew).
BORAGE: Attracts bees and wasps.
CARAWAY: Attracts tiny parasitic wasps. Competes with dill and fennel.
DILL: Attracts hoverflies and predatory wasps, which prey on pests. Avoid near carrots and tomatoes, as they also attract hornworms and swallowtail caterpillars.
LAVENDER; Attracts bees.
MINT: Attract hoverflies, predatory wasps, and earthworms.
NASTURTIUM: Attracts predatory insects, including ladybugs.
OREGANO: Attracts pollinators.
PARSLEY: Dropped seeds attract tiny parasitic wasps and hoverflies.
RED CLOVER: Attracts bees.
SAGE: Attracts pollinators.
SUNFLOWERS: Attract pollinators.

GREAT REPELLERS:

BORAGE: Deters cabbage worm and tomato hornworm.

CATNIP: Deters aphids, flea beetles, Japanese beetles, squash-bugs, ants and weevils.

CHERVIL: Deters aphids from lettuce. May deter slugs.

CHIVES: Deters slugs from lettuce and strawberries, carrot rust fly, and aphids. Avoid near beans and peas.

CHRYSANTHEMUMS: C. coccineum kills root nema-todes. White flowering mums repel Japanese beetles.

CLOVER: Attracts predators of the woolly aphid and interferes with the colonization of cabbage worms and aphids. Also attracts predator ground beetles.

COMFREY: Attracts (traps) slugs.

DILL: Repels aphids, spider mites, squash bug.

FEVERFEW: High in pyrethrum, repels even bees. Toxic to cats. A good insect repellent if you rub leaves on skin.

FOUR-O'CLOCKS: Attracts Japanese beetles, who are poisoned by eating their leaves. Toxic to humans and pets.

GARLIC: Repels aphids, borers, snails, and some flies.

GERANIUM: Repels cabbage worms and Japanese beetles.

HORSERADISH: Repels blister beetles and Colorado potato beetle.

HOREHOUND: Attract Braconid and Icheumonid wasps, and Tachnid and Syrid flies, parasitic to pests.

HYSSOP: Deters cabbage moths and flea beetles. Avoid near radishes.

LAMIUM: Repels potato bugs.

LARKSPUR: Attracts and poisons Japanese beetles.

LAVENDER: Repels fleas and moths (codling/fruit pests).

LEMON BALM: Citronella repels mosquitoes and squash bugs.

MARIGOLDS: Kill bad nemotodes, but do attract spider mites and slugs. Deters whitefly, bean beetle, and rabbits. Mexican marigold is the most potent. Avoid near beans and cabbage.

MINT: Deters ants, aphids, flea beetles, fleas, squash bugs, rodents, and white cabbage moths.

NASTURTIUM: Attracts (traps) black aphids. Deters squash bugs, striped pumpkin beetles, wooly aphids, whiteflies, cucumber beetles and other pests of the cucurbit family.

OREGANO: Repels cabbage butterfly and cucumber beetle.

PARSLEY: Repels asparagus beetles. Keep away from mint.

SUNFLOWER: Attracts (traps) aphids. Ants will herd them onto stalks.

Recommended Reading:

15 Minute Field Trips blog:
  www.15minutefieldtrips.blogspot.com
Animal, Vegetable, Miracle by Barbara Kingsolver
Around the World in 100 Miles blog:
  www.aroundtheworldin100miles.blogspot.com
Ball Complete Book of Home Preserving: 400 Delicious
  and Creative Recipes for Today by Judi Kingry and
  Lauren Devine
Celebrating the Great Mother Cait Johnson and Maura
  D. Shaw
Family Herbal Rosemary Gladstar
Food, Inc. Katl Weber, Editor
Golden Harvest Organics: www.ghorganics.com
In Defense of Food Michael Polland
Living Like Ed Ed Begley Jr.
The Omnivore's Dilemma Michael Polland
Stirring It Up Gary Hirshberg

Glossary:

Cage-Free Animals have access to the outside, anywhere from free range of pasture to an open door onto pavement.

CSA Community Supported Agriculture. Individuals and families can pre-pay for a share of a farm, receiving weekly bags of produce. Some CSAs also include eggs, dairy, and meat.

Co-Op A business, often a grocery, supported by a cooperation, where individuals supply funding and volunteer hours and share in the products.

Cow-Share Buying a whole cow with other people with the intention of dividing the cost and parts. Similarly, **Pig-Share**.

Certified Organic Foods that have been grown without chemical or artificial pesticides, in soil free from contaminants for at least three years. Oregon Tilth certifies most operations. A farm may still use organic practices without being officially certified; just ask. Also, consider the carbon food-print: organic carrots from your local farm or California? Organic kiwis from the Artic kiwis now grown in New England or New Zealand kiwis?

Free-Range Livestock are allowed to roam outside cages and pens, getting light and air, mixed greens, and insects into their diet. Eggs have lower cholesterol and yellower yolks. Animals have better health.

IPM Integrated Pest Management. Using timing, companion planting, beneficial insects, traps, and nature-derived sprays to manage problems with pests. Ask your orchard farmer if they practice this.

Pasture-Finished Animal has fed in a pasture until slaughter. Animal was not fed a diet of corn and antibiotics, but what the animal would naturally eat.

Volunteer You, possibly? People who share their time and skills to better their community, digging gardens, teaching classes, cleaning beaches, picking up someone else's trash, making posters, making calls, and paying it forward. Get out there!

Index: